TWAYNE'S WORLD LEADERS SERIES

Arnold Toynbee

Arnold Toynbee

Arnold Toynbee

The Ecumenical Vision

KENNETH WINETROUT

American International College

TWAYNE PUBLISHERS

A DIVISION OF G. K. HALL & CO., BOSTON

Copyright © 1975 G. K. Hall & Co.

All Rights Reserved

Library of Congress Cataloging in Publication Data

Winetrout, Kenneth.
  Arnold Toynbee: the ecumenical vision.

  (Twayne's world leaders series)
  Bibliography: p. 139-52.
  1. Toynbee, Arnold Joseph, 1889-   A study of history.
2. Toynbee, Arnold Joseph, 1889-   3. Civilization.
4. History—Philosophy. I. Title. CB63.T68W56   907'.2'024
(B)   74-17162 ISBN 0-8057-3725-1

MANUFACTURED IN THE UNITED STATES OF AMERICA

Contents

About the Author

Kenneth Winetrout, Margaret C. Ells Professor of Education, has been at American International College, Springfield, Massachusetts, since 1948. Previous to coming to his present position he taught in the public schools of Ohio and Puerto Rico and taught creative writing at Stephens College. He has served as visiting professor at Smith, Mount Holyoke, Wesleyan and Trinity colleges, the University of Arkansas and Washington University. He is the author of *F.C.S. Schiller and the Dimensions of Pragmatism*, and a contributor to *The New Sociology* and to *Sight, Sound, and Society*. He is co-author of the monograph *Bureaucrats and Intellectuals: A Critique of C. Wright Mills*. His articles have appeared in over 35 journals including *The Bulletin of the Atomic Scientists, The Christian Century, ETC, Journal of Individual Psychology, Journal of Thought*, and *The Personalist*.

Preface

There are no more deserts. There are no more islands. Yet one still feels the need of them. To understand this world, one must sometimes turn away from it; to serve men better, one must briefly hold them at a distance. But where can the necessary solitude be found, the long breathing space in which the mind gathers its strength and takes stock of its courage? There are still the great cities. But they must meet certain conditions. The cities of Europe are too full of murmurs from the past. The practiced ear can still detect the rustling of wings, the quivering of souls. We feel the dizziness of the centuries, of glory and revolutions. We are reminded of the clamor in which Europe was forged. There is not enough silence.

Albert Camus in *Lyrical and Critical Essays*

Of all historians, Toynbee most overwhelms his reader with "murmurs from the past"; in him, the reader encounters the "dizziness of the centuries." Be it an obscure city in a remote area of Asia or a city out of the remote past with scarcely an archaeological remnant in site, Toynbee brings the historical past down on the reader in a torrent of erudite allusions. As he views Balkh, one of the ancient capital cities of the Kushan Empire, he is "awe-stricken": "Those giant mud walls and towers and mounds give, even in their present decay, a visual sense of the momentum of human effort on the grand scale sustained over a span of dozens of centuries."[1]

While Camus would have some silence from the past, Toynbee seems to be in love with its clamorings and whisperings. He comes to us drenched with historical lore; and as he looks out over the world landscape, he envelops virtually all its features with commentaries on its past. Toynbee magnifies the difficulty for his reader by giving an almost equivalent range of observations from the immediate present. For Toynbee, there are no deserts, no islands, no silence, and he is in love with this condition.

In Toynbee, the ecumenical and the minutiae coalesce. He will toy with an incident or a place that is seemingly known only to Toynbee. He will play games with civilizations and religions in a manner at times suggestive of the cavalier treatment of a political candidate toward his opponent. The reader is tossed about on a sea of infinite detail and metaphysical theorizing of the highest order.

The challenge is formidable. Bertrand Russell has said that it has become correct to praise Plato but not to understand him. Toynbee has already approximated this position, but with a difference: it has become customary to praise, or to dismiss, him but not to understand him. Toynbee is in bulk just too much, and the easy way out is to dismiss him; indeed, enough eminent men have so treated him that the ordinary reader is not hard put to rationalize his own dismissal of Toynbee. Dismissal becomes a posture of self-defense. And if one persists in trying to understand Toynbee, perhaps one does so at the cost of "psychic numbing." (The term is Robert Jay Lifton's for man's response to nuclear war.)

We have become too accustomed to microscope-using historians. Toynbee's historical instrument is neither a microscope nor yet a pair of field glasses; his is the telescope; a kind of private telescope which he has set up in his own backyard for his own use. The reader is not privileged to look through this telescope; rather he is told what Toynbee sees. Toynbee writes: "I am trying to use our knowledge of history as a telescope-lens for taking a look at the universe as a whole."[2] We have the observation: a hundred-inch telescope is not designed for surveying the frontyard.

If a telescope is not very well adapted for looking at the grass on the front lawn, it could follow that the eye behind the telescope lens may see neither the grass nor the men cutting the grass nor the men making love and waging war. A number of persons have commented that Toynbee's intended audience is not his contemporaries. William Kaufmann says he wrote for generations hence. George Catlin holds that Toynbee has the charming quirk of writing as if his reader were in A.D. 2052.

One may get this impression of a distant, far-in-the-future audience. Yet the truth is that Toynbee has addressed himself more aggressively and more fundamentally to the issues of his day than most historians. War and racism are recurring themes in A Study of History as well as in his single volume works. Poverty amid affluence is a pervasive theme. Toynbee's view is universal, taking in the past and the present.

One can never be quite sure where to begin a discussion on Toynbee, where to cut in on this amorphous bulk, this ecumenical resume with asides tossed in on his Uncle William and Aunt Grace. Nor can one be quite sure where to end. The massiveness of his writings and the indecision about where to begin and where to end leaves dismissal as an ever-inviting prospect.

But dismissal has scarcely been Toynbee's fate. He continues to write books and make headlines with random comments on this or that issue. He continues to inspire in others both adulation and disgust. At this moment we see two indications of his viability in the publishing world. In 1973, an English translation of Jose Ortega y Gasset's *An Interpretation of Universal History* was published by W.W. Norton. And also in 1973 there appeared another voluminous condensation of Toynbee's A *Study of History* (this one edited by Arnold Toynbee and Jane Caplan).

This much we know: Toynbee takes his reader on a long long journey through space and time and perhaps fantasy. The vistas vary: some appear to be pure wastelands, whereas others suggest an exotic Garden of Eden. There are many Toynbees in Toynbee, but in the end they all add up to a marvelous single being. In the words of Rousseau's *Autobiography,* we may say of Toynbee as Rousseau once said of Rousseau, there is no other like Arnold Toynbee and surely by now God has destroyed the mold.

While it may be true that some books are their own excuse for being, it seems to me that the present writer owes his reader a brief explanation of how this book came about. It is scarcely by accident that one comes to read the whole of A *Study of History.* My introduction to Arnold Toynbee came in the fall of 1955. Scott Buchanan, who with Stringfellow Barr founded the Great Books program at St. John's College, was giving a year-long seminar (1955–56) on Toynbee at Springfield College, and the text for the seminar was A *Study of History*—all ten volumes. Without the late Scott Buchanan's scholarly and delightful approach to Toynbee, this volume would never have been begun—or completed.

Some of Dr. Buchanan's remarks remain with me. I recall his saying something very much to this effect: historians find Toynbee an excellent philosopher but a terrible historian; philosophers see in him an excellent historian but a most unsatisfactory philosopher. Dr. Buchanan once left us with this cryptic comment: "If I had read Toynbee before going to St. John's, the Great Books program would have been quite different." None of us ever pressed him on precisely what he meant by this, but this seemed certain: the reading of Toynbee had had a profound influence on the way Scott Buchanan viewed history, philosophy, and education.

If memory does not mislead me, Dr. Buchanan was simultaneously giving Toynbee seminars in Washington, D.C., Pittsfield, Mass., as well as the one I attended in Springfield, Mass. One can only marvel that a single person would ever attempt a second seminar on *A Study of History* whether given simultaneously or sequentially. But Scott Buchanan conducted our seminar with freshness, charm, and the benefit of Greek scholarship.

Ever since that seminar it has seemed to me unfortunate that no one had seen fit to undertake a book-length examination of Arnold Toynbee. (Ortega y Gasset's book is more Ortega y Gasset than Toynbee and falls far short of giving a comprehensive view of the major themes in *A Study.*) I can readily appreciate why others have not taken on this task. For one thing, the sheer mass is enough to frighten off all but the most foolhardy. Indeed, one may suppose that no single writer will ever come up with the definitive book on Arnold Toynbee; such a work is likely to result only from the collective effort of a group of scholars.

The present volume makes no pretense of being more than an introduction to the major themes in *A Study of History.* Whole areas of Toynbee's scholarly effort receive scant or no attention. The reader will find but the most cursory commentary on Toynbee as a historian of the Graeco-Roman period; likewise there is little discussion of his work in British intelligence. What we have here is not a book for the historian *qua* historian but rather an attempt at intellectual biography for the general reader. It is a book in which Toynbee does much of the talking. To some, the documentation may seem excessive and inhibitory; but it seemed important to me that the reader should be able to locate this or that observation, this or that theme, without getting lost in a search through what is literally millions of words. The long quotations may show what a delightful stylist Toynbee can be on occasion and again on other occasions what a severe burden he can put on his reader.

Preface

Toynbee is eminently worthy of a book and not just reviews and essays in books however numerous these may be; and further, this book was written in the hope that others might be encouraged to read him. Far too much has already been written that has the effect of dissuading one from turning directly or even indirectly to *A Study of History.* Whatever may be the limitations of Toynbee on whatever score, genuine rewards and pleasures will come to him who takes up the unabridged work. This enormity is an exercise in frustration: the voluminousness, the erudition, and the grand generalities are overwhelming. But one comes away from this immersion in the ecumenical Dr. Toynbee with an enrichment and an enlargement of perspective. For this, and this alone if necessary, let us be grateful for Arnold J. Toynbee.

During the fall of 1955 and into the winter of 1956 I was reading thirty hours or more a week in *A Study.* One cannot devote this amount of time and at the same time teach a full college load without the cooperation of one's family. Lacking the kind indulgence of my wife Julia and the understanding manners of Mark and Nancy, a seminar and a volume on Toynbee would have been impossible. To them, as always, my gratitude and my affection.

A generous thank you goes to Carole Ardison, Beverly Faille, and Jean Stefanik for their help in preparing the manuscript.

It has been a pleasure to work under the editorship of Arthur W. Brown, Baruch College, and Thomas S. Knight, Adelphi University; both have been helpful and encouraging editors.

* * *

My grandfather John F. Ricker was born June 30, 1852, on a farm near Galion, Ohio. He was born as a divided nation began preparations for the Civil War. His death came in 1941 in the month of Pearl Harbor. My grandson Christopher Steven Winetrout was born June 30, 1973, in Schenectady, New York. If mankind survives the evils of war, racism, affluence, pollution, and overpopulation—all given much attention by Toynbee—then on June 30, 2052, I expect Christopher Steven to celebrate his 79th birthday and the bicentennial of his great great grandfather Ricker. This volume is dedicated to these two members of my family who together give me a two-centuries personal stake in the cosmos. I think Arnold Toynbee would understand this dedication.

KENNETH WINETROUT

American International College

Chronology

1889 Arnold J. Toynbee born in London, April 14, son of Harry
V. Toynbee and Sarah Edith Marshall. His paternal grandfather had been London's first ear, nose, and throat
specialist. His father worked for a short time with a tea-
importing firm, but soon left that to join the staff of the
Charity Organization Society. His mother was an historian.
Toynbee writes: "By middle-class standards, my parents
were poor, yet they always had a cook and a housemaid 'living in' and employed full-time. When I was born, they engaged a nurse for me in addition."

1899 Entered Wootton Court, a boarding school, and remained
there for three years.

1902 Enrolled at Winchester and left there in 1907. "For five
years at Winchester, I had tasted what life had been like
for Primitive Man. One found oneself suddenly plunged
into a world of arbitrary prohibitions and commandments."

1907 Studied classics at Balliol College, Oxford, taking his degree in 1911.

1909 Studied under Sir Alfred Zimmern, the author of *The
Greek Commonwealth*. Zimmern threw up "any number of
bridges over the time-gulf between the Greeks' history and
ours. Evidently his interest in the Graeco-Roman World
did not rule out a parallel interest in the present-day
world."

1911 Studied at the British Archaeological School in Athens.

1912 Married Rosalind Murray, the daughter of Gilbert Murray,
distinguished professor of classics at Oxford. This marriage
ended in divorce in 1945.

1912 Served as tutor at Balliol College until 1915.

1915 Became an amanuensis for Lord Bryce with the purpose of
assembling and writing *The Treatment of Armenians in the
Ottoman Empire 1915–16*. In a letter to Viscount Grey

Lord Bryce wrote: "I had the good fortune to secure the co-operation of a young historian of high academic distinction, Mr. Arnold J. Toynbee, late fellow of Balliol College, Oxford."

1915 Joined the Political Intelligence Department of the Foreign Office and served in that office until 1919. Health kept Toynbee from serving in the armed services.

1919 Attended the Paris Peace Conference. Among those he met in Paris was Col. T. E. Lawrence.

1919 Held the Koraes Chair of Byzantine and Modern Greek Studies at London University. Resigned in 1924.

1924 Toynbee began 33 years as Director of Studies at Chatham House and produced the voluminous *Survey of International Affairs*. "From 1924 to 1956 I was producing the *Survey of International Affairs* at Chatham House in partnership with my wife. From 1927 to 1954 I was producing the first ten volumes of *A Study of History*. From all points of view this was, for me, a most happy combination of activities. I do not believe I could have produced either the *Survey* or the *Study* if I had not been at work on both of them simultaneously. Together they gave me the widest horizon that I was capable of attaining." Continued to lecture at London University.

1929 First visit to India and China.

1934 Volumes I–III of *A Study of History* published.

1936 Met Hitler while in Germany to deliver a lecture before the Nazi Law Society. Toynbee was criticized for making this trip; "I had defended my acceptance (invitation to deliver lecture) by pointing out that to study the Nazi was an important part of my job at Chatham House. How could I study them without meeting them?" He listened to one of Hitler's two-hour lectures. During the lecture he was intent on Hitler's hands. "He had beautiful hands." Toynbee's comment that "the Nazi surely broke mankind's previous record for meanness" makes his position on the Nazis unmistakably clear.

1939 Volumes IV–VI of *A Study of History* published.

1946 Married Veronica Boulter, a research associate at Chatham House. Soon they formed a partnership of equals in writing the *Survey of International Affairs:* "Our minds proved to match each other. To this day, if I open some volume of our *Survey* at random and glance at the page, I am unable, as often as not, to tell whether that page was Veronica's work or mine." The partnership continued after their retirement from Chatham House: "Since our retirement, she still continues to make the indexes for all my books."

1946 Attended the second Paris Peace Conference. "I am not the only person in my generation who has attended two Paris Peace conferences. There are several of us who shared with each other this uncanny and disquieting experience." Twenty-seven years passed between the two conferences, and Toynbee asked if twenty-seven years was the Paris-peace-conference wave-length! "If it is, we shall be back again in 1973; and that is a horrifying thought; for, in order to have a Paris peace conference, one has first to have a world war." It is interesting to note that Henry Kissinger was in Paris in 1973.

1954 Volumes VII–X of *A Study of History* published.

1959 Volume XI *Historical Atlas and Gazetteer* published.

1960 Volume XII *Reconsiderations* published.

1969 The autobiographical *Experiences* published. Toynbee concludes that volume with a "Posthumous Agenda." Toynbee declared himself totally involved in the future. For one thing, there are now sixteen persons in his immediate family. "I am involved in mankind's future, whatever its future may prove to be; and I am also involved in what will happen to the Universe after mankind has become extinct, supposing extinction is mankind's eventual fate." This is one way of saying that with Toynbee, no chronology ever ends.

CHAPTER 1

Toynbee as Historian

T HERE is not much one can say to prepare the reader for his encounter with *A Study of History*. Toynbee is unlike any other historian. *A Study of History* is unlike any other book in the field of history—nor are there any equivalents in other disciplines. Christopher Dawson says it is "the most massive work that our generation has seen or is likely to see." Massiveness is one thing, but universalistic massiveness is something else, and throughout prophecy is piled atop prophecy. Dawson sees Toynbee motivated by two goals: the Hellenic philosophic quest for a "synoptic vision of the whole course of human civilization" and "by the Hebraic prophetic mission to justify the ways of God to man and to find a religious solution to the riddle of history."[1]

Earlier Hegel had marked off what this sort of ambition implied.

A history which aspires to traverse long periods of time, or to be universal, must indeed forego the attempt to give individual representations of the past as it actually existed. It must foreshorten its pictures by abstractions; and this includes not merely the omission of events and deeds, but whatever is involved in the fact that thought is, after all, the most trenchant epitomist. A battle, a great victory, a siege, no longer maintains its original proportions, but is put off with a bare mention.[2]

But Toynbee never intended and never does allow these Hegelian restraints to condition his work. He does not foreshorten his history with abstractions; for, in truth, individual events are present in the fullness of multitudinous array. Kaufmann finds *A Study* a "supercolossus" performance with a "cast of thousands ranging from churches and civilizations to the author and his family."[3] Catlin is succinct: "Everything is included, from Hammurabi to 'my Aunt Grace.' "[4]

There is endless erudition. We have here a historian who looks with scorn at the "tiny allotments" other "historical specialists" have assigned themselves.[5] We find him arranging his cast of thousands, shifting his scenery from a framed picture in his grandfather's house to the world at large, acting now as a "Hebrew prophet," now as a "Catholic in the Middle Ages," and still again as a "Christian Buddhist."[6]

Robert Lifton has described modern man as a protean character, as one who plays many roles. Toynbee is the protean historian, and yet he is not the protean man.

I

Many persons must have asked themselves what in the name of heaven could ever inspire or provoke a man in this century to undertake and complete a thirteen-volume study of history? And although some of us may wish for a more candid answer, some for a more thorough one, and some for a shorter one, everyone must admit that Toynbee does tell us why he wrote *A Study*.

For a man who deals in thousand-year cycles, who has played mortician to some twenty civilizations, Toynbee's first reason is sweet and tender: he wrote this opus because of his mother. Philip Wylie might want to make something of this, but I think any Wylie diagnosis at this point would be irrelevant. Toynbee is simply giving credit to family influences. He concludes the preface to the first edition with this tribute: "Finally, the writer cannot lay down his pen without mentioning one earliest debt of all . . . which he owes his Mother, who first turned his thoughts towards History by being a historian herself."[7] He gives a somewhat longer tribute in his essay "My View of History":

There are many angles of vision from which human minds peer at the universe. Why am I a historian, not a philosopher or a physicist? For the same reason I drink tea and coffee without sugar. Both habits were formed at a tender age by following a lead from my mother. I am a historian because my mother was one before me; yet at the same time I am conscious that I am of a different school from her.[8]

Further, Toynbee considers himself fortunate in the historians and scholars he has known as friends. They too turned him in the direction of history. Persons met here and there in his travels also encouraged him in this endeavor. Much of volume ten is given over to tributes to associates, to authors of books which influenced his thinking, to those who took the trouble to correspond with him. *Acquaintances* is a book-length tribute to those he has known along a widely traveled path. His credit lines to those who differed with him are models of decorum.

There are times when Toynbee is pleased to give very short answers to why he has spent his lifetime in studying history: "My answer is 'for fun.' I find this an adequate answer, and it is certainly a sincere one."[9] And he is ever ready to assure us that if he had to live his life over, he would spend it in the same way. Again: "Why work, and why at history? Because, for me, this is the pursuit that leads, however haltingly, towards the *Visio Beatifica.*"[10]

These brief replies have a certain appeal and we may accept that Toynbee gives such answers in candor and sincerity. But we must look further for deeper reasons, and we discover a good deal of this when we examine what Toynbee finds wrong in other histories. History in the large is deficient in the eyes of Toynbee because of an inherent parochialism. The Western historian is too much caught up in his own narrow view; he is remiss in his unconcern about the East. One catches some of this in the way the word "natives" has been used in the West. We see "natives" as "trees walking, or as wild animals," as "parts of the local flora and fauna." We fail to see them as men with passions like ours, and as a result we treat them as though they "did not possess ordinary human rights."[11]

The Westernized version of history has its basis in the economic and political impact European and American forces have made on the rest of the world. Technology in our time has brought about a seemingly unified world. This, Toynbee warns, is an illusion. Beneath the economic and political strata there exists a fundamental stratum which Toynbee calls the cultural. Commercial and military penetrations occur easily, but at the cultural level a non-Western civilization is much more resistant to Western penetrations.

The economic and political maps have been "Westernized," but beneath these there remain the deeper cultural maps, which are largely untouched by Western conquest or intervention. Even the Western steamroller has not been able to blot out "the fainter outlines of the frail primitive societies." We Westerners use the word "native" as a piece of smoked glass in order "that the gratifying spectacle of a 'Westernized' surface may not be disturbed by any perception of the native fires which are still blazing underneath."[12]

In his essay "The Unification of the World" we find our historian further elaborating on this theme: "The paradox of our generation is that all the world has now profited by an education which the West has provided, except the West itself. The West today is still looking at history from that old parochial self-centred standpoint which other living societies have by now been compelled to transcend."[13] But sooner or later (and sooner we gather is the hope of Toynbee) we are going to have to come around to a less parochial outlook. The day is coming when we will be living in a world which will be "neither Western nor non-Western," but which will be made up of "all the cultures which we Westerners have now brewed together in a single crucible."[14] Our descendants will be the heirs of Confucius, Lao-Tse, and Buddha and not just of Plato, Christ, and Paul. All of this means a readjustment in historical outlook, and this readjustment may be by far the most difficult for us in the West, unless we overcome our narrow point of view in history.

In one of Toynbee's most personal essays, "A Study of History: What I Am Trying to Do," we get some further insight into just what it is he is trying to do in writing history, or, if one should prefer, in rewriting history. He wants to incorporate the East into our heritage. This would seem to be a major shortcoming in our history writing. "In that antiquated Late Modern Western picture there is no room at all for China or India."[15] We must give up this pattern; we are going to have to see history "with new eyes."

One can only applaud Toynbee in his attack upon Western parochialism; one is grateful for his efforts to incorporate the Hindu, the Moslem, and the Hittite into our view of history. However, all of this inclusiveness and pluralism seems weakened by Toynbee's effort to make all history subservient to a single force, namely, religion. Toynbee, it seems to me, does us a great and needed service in asserting our plural sources; but he does us and his history a disservice when in the face of this concept of pluralistic origins, he insists on a single destination. If we may assign a plurality of causal origins, then may we not by the same justification assign a plurality of destinations? Toynbee is gener-

ous on origin and stingy on destiny. There would seem to be little or no advantage in assuming multiple causation, if one is then
denied the freedom of postulating multiple effects. Toynbee,
though, remains the poet laureate of deo-tropism, and this is
scarcely the appropriate time to engage in a discussion of this
particular tropism. One can perhaps tarry long enough to wonder
with William James: What is so wonderful and sacred about one?
What is wrong with 101, 201, or even 2001?

If there is any everpresent thorn in the historical skin of Arnold
Toynbee, it is nationalism. Parochialism is a generalized sin;
nationalism is a particular sin. One of Toynbee's aims as a historian or as a prophet or as a metaphysician is to discover what
he calls an "intelligible unit of history." The nation is clearly too
small and insignificant to serve as this. This is one of his quarrels
with nationalism but only a part of his quarrel.

Nationalism is a perversion, the idolization of a ghost. It is a
cause of war. Over and over Toynbee reminds us it is this
nation-bias that impairs the possibility of writing good history.
Here Toynbee differs sharply with so many other historians, and
here he becomes the target of some of the most bitter criticism.
Nationalism perverts whole peoples as well as individual historians: "The spirit of Nationality is a sour ferment of the new
wine of Democracy in the old bottles of Tribalism."[16] Toynbee
sees the modern world as under the domination of nationalism
and industrialism rather than under democracy and industrialism.

Historians have welcomed nationalism because it fits in so well
with their concept of the division of labor. It allows scholars to
specialize. In this fashion one becomes an authority on English
history, French history, German history, etc. This pattern of writing history came along about the same time as the industrial revolution, which stressed the division of labor and nationalism.
Toynbee has this little dig at the French historian Camille Jullian:
"Into however distant a past he travels back, he carries France
with him—contented if he can do so with ease, embarrassed if he
cannot do so without difficulty, but ever incapable of leaving
France behind him."[17] One supposes that in Jullian's frame of
reference there will always be a France even four thousand years
before there existed a France.

In no small part, then, Toynbee took up his pen to write his
study because he could not stomach the nationalistic bias of historical scholarship.

Another of his dislikes is what he calls "the industrialization of historical writing." This industrialization had gone so far that one found in histories "the pathological exaggeration of the industrial spirit."[18] The assembling of raw materials became a goal. It did not matter that these assembled facts might never be used in a creative or unified manner. It was a production problem. Historians piled up the facts and then accepted praise for the massiveness of their stockpiling virtuosity. A chief sinner in this regard, according to Toynbee, was Theodor Mommsen: "Mommsen made it his life work to organize the exhaustive publication of Latin inscriptions and the encyclopaedic presentation of Roman Constitutional Law."[19]

The proliferation of monographs results from this approach to history. One monograph after another appeared in the learned periodicals without any relationship to each other: "Those periodicals were the Industrial System 'in book form' with its division of labor and its sustained maximum output of articles manufactured from raw materials mechanically."[20]

Toynbee accuses historians of busying themselves in raking over any old rubbish heap for data and then "bringing the stuff out of the wholesalers' warehouses in the bulk and retailing it to the public in an infinite number of infinitesimally small samples."[21]

Historians have been inhibited from joining other disciplines in finding "laws of nature." Others have found that the greater the quantity of data, the greater was the precision with which laws of nature, universal laws, might be ascertained. Historians, in contrast to other scholars, suffered from the delusion that "the panorama of History was incomprehensibly complex."[22]

The industrial revolution with its division of labor and its emphasis on production for the sake of production gave the historian an unfortunate model in the nineteenth century. Another movement from this past century, natural science, also had an adverse effect on history. This was the century of Darwin, Huxley, and Spencer, and the historian began to imitate the scientist. Toynbee is annoyed by these efforts to imitate the naturalist. He finds their seminars "laboratories": "When a professor of history calls his 'seminar' a 'laboratory', he is not wilfully expatriating himself from his natural environment."[23] Taine was one historian who took natural science as a model. The historian, declared Taine, has to act like a naturalist and free himself from "all personal predilections and all moral standards." He likens the moralist to a botanist who studies with equal interest the orange tree, the laurel, the pine, the beech. The historian becomes a kind of botanist who deals with the works of man rather than plants.[24]

This is what Toynbee calls the "apathetic fallacy": "We are sufficiently on our guard against the so-called 'Pathetic Fallacy' of imaginatively endowing inanimate objects with life. We now fall victims to the inverse 'Apathetic Fallacy' of treating living things as though they were inanimate."[25]

Toynbee, it seems safe to assume, began to write *A Study* because he wished to overcome the shortcomings he found in the work of other historians: the inexcusable parochialism of the Western writer; the distortions which the Western blinders created; the omnipresent nationalism; the patterning of history after an industrial model; the stockpiling of data and resultant monographic productions; and the imitation of the natural scientist. Toynbee would have the historian be neither the industrialist nor yet the botanist. These things, then, annoyed him; his mother and associates inspired him.

Beyond the negative elements of motivation which we have been examining, we must find some positive reasons for Toynbee's embarking on this massive opus. Two digging operations in the present century had considerable impact on Toynbee. The excavations of archaeologists pushed the time frontier of the historian further and further into the past. While the digging went on in Greece, Turkey, India, Yucatan, and elsewhere, another kind of archaeology was being discovered in Vienna and Zurich, where Freud, Adler, Jung, and others were probing into dreams and discovering myths and collective representations which hinted at a very distant past inherent in man.

In the process of attaining a new unity, the world has grown immensely larger. When we began the present century, "our historical horizon in the West was virtually limited to Israel, Greece, and Rome." Archaeologists have since extended our horizons in both space and time. We now know the whole face of our planet; and we can look backward in time, not a mere 5,000 or 6,000 years but perhaps even 1,000,000 years. In a similar manner, psychologists have expanded our realm to include "the psyche's unfathomable subconscious abyss." History becomes a unity; and we can see "all aspects of human life as so many facets of a unitary human nature."[26] All of this became most welcome grist for Toynbee's ecumenical mill.

Shortly after completing the first ten volumes, Toynbee expressed a fear that his book might soon be out of date: "I seem to catch the faint sound of the busy archaeologist's trowel . . . and the psychologists are digging down deeper. A student of history will never find himself out of work, so long as he keeps his wits."[27]

Toynbee frequently credits archaeology with prompting him to write his history. He sees a "new model army of Western archaeologists" joined with Western orientalists marching shoulder to shoulder "in an intellectual crusade against a parochial-minded native Western ignorance."[28] This same army "had increased the number of civilizations known to Western scholars sevenfold, from a trio to more than a score." To Toynbee this represents an immense enlargement of the West's historical horizon. This crusade had "put the historian to rout." He views the work of the archaeologist as decisive in the field of history as the Germans had been in the military.

Psychology and archaeology joined forces to give us a unified concept of man. In a sense, Schliemann and Freud were playing the same game by pulling a distant past together. We thus begin to see man in universal terms. In a somewhat similar way technology and economics are pulling the present together. Industrialism also presupposes a worldwide approach to things. What we have is a new inclusiveness: "This deep impulse to envisage and comprehend the whole of life is certainly immanent in the mind of the historian."[29] We need to look at history with new eyes, and for Toynbee this means with eyes that see the total landscape. He aspires to be the historian with the widest possible perspective: "The governing idea is the familiar one that the universe becomes intelligible to the extent of our ability to apprehend it as a whole."[30]

And even this world is not enough. We include in our hypothesis the kingdom of heaven, and with this history passes over into theology.

The quarrel many historians have with Toynbee is that Toynbee, while posing as an historian, constantly slips over into playing the theologian. To encompass the whole is to approximate both cosmology and theology. Needless to say, most historians

are willing to stop short of Toynbee's cosmic and theological aspirations. Toynbee goes the full route: "Our first task is to per-
ceive, and to present to other people, the history of all known
civilizations, surviving and extinct, as a unity."[31]

If we come to think of history as a unified process, a bus in
which all peoples travel down the same road in time toward the
same destiny, then prophecy and doom take on a new significance. If civilization is, on the other hand, a house of many mansions, then one or two of these mansions may burn down with
less tragic results. Having put all mankind into one hopper,
Toynbee is forced by his own devices to play prophet and to take
a good look at doom.

In our period every citizen in the West with any sense of history must entertain the possibility that Western civilization has
already "entered on the path of disintegration," and that there is
no turning back, no chance of reversing the trend.[32]

To write history as theology and prophecy there must be, says
Toynbee, an intelligible unit of history. The nation is utterly inadequate and unacceptable on this ground. For six volumes in *A
Study* Tonybee leads his reader to believe this intelligible unit is
to be found in the concept civilization: "I mean by civilization the
smallest unit of historical study at which one arrives when one
tries to understand this history of one's own country."[33] About
halfway through volume seven Toynbee, without any direct warning to his reader, announces that civilization as an intelligible unit
just will not work. Instead, he claims that henceforth the intelligible unit must be religion. This is the big switch in *A Study*.

Toynbee does not hesitate to let us know that he was not the
first to reach this conclusion. Herodotus and Rashid-ad-Din, who
first asked what is this world, arrived at the conclusion that "no
field smaller than the entire Oikoumene since the dawn of history
is an intelligible field of historical study."[34] Another reason, then,
for writing *A Study* is this self-appointed task of discovering an
intelligible unit of historical study.

Personal irritations also must be reckoned as a motive force
helping to bring *A Study* into existence. Over and over Toynbee
names Edward Gibbon as one of the great historians of all times.
One cannot question this admiration for Gibbon, and yet Gibbon
never allowed Toynbee to sleep soundly. In a sense, Gibbon is
Toynbee's troubled conscience: "A large part of his ten volumes

may be said to be a response to the challenge of Gibbon."[35] Nor
did Toynbee let up with the completion of the ten volumes. In
Volume XII, *Reconsiderations,* Toynbee is still struggling with
Gibbon. Here we read that Gibbon "was a genius who was
rationalist-minded to an almost naively un-self-critical degree."[36]
This rationalist bent in Gibbon made for his mistaken notions
about the role religions play in peoples and civilizations.

The problems of war and class have played a part in inspiring *A
Study:* "We are thus confronted with a challenge our predeces-
sors never had to face. We have to abolish War and Class—and
abolish them now—under pain, if we flinch or fail, of seeing them
win a victory over man which, this time, would be conclusive and
definitive."[37] Nuclear warfare is the new dimension.

Toynbee, like F.S.C. Northrop in *The Meeting of East and
West,* wants to bring about better relationships between East and
West: "The ordinary man today wants to know about these great
world societies which have now become the protagonists in the
historical drama and the ordinary history book does very little to
help him. That is the obvious justification for Dr. Toynbee's
study and one of the main reasons for its wide popularity."[38]

In this age a cosmic prophet and a universal historian must
present his credentials. Toynbee willingly puts his on the table.
He was born at the right time—1889. Had he been born later, he
would have missed that classical education so necessary in his as-
piration to be a universal historian. He was educated "almost entirely in the Greek and Roman Classics." For any would-be historian, "a classical education is a priceless boon." There are
reasons for this pride in a classical education. For one thing, the
Graeco-Roman period is over; hence we can see it in the perspective of the whole. Further, it is manageable in terms of the
amount of material on hand to study. We are not lost in a
superabundance of data. We can, as it were, still see the forest.
The materials from the classical period come to us well balanced:
a fine proportion of poetry, philosophy, science, and law. And
there is a third ingredient very important to Toynbee—the ecumenical tone so characteristic of the classical period in contrast to
the parochial tone which dominates most other historical periods.

The classical education gives him one dimension of what he
calls his "binocular view of history." His classical education made
him a Hellenist. The other part of his vision comes from his very

contemporary work at Chatham House: here he literally dealt with events as they happened: "Two divergent forces in the historian's social milieu—current events and an Hellenic education—were thus always simultaneously exerting themselves upon his line of thought, and these divergent forces found their resolution in his mind in a habit of looking at history as a series of comparisons in two terms."[39] He could always ask himself: what would Churchill have done in Athens? What would Pericles have done in London? Whatever the issue, Toynbee brought two pair of eyes to it: Hellenic and modern. Toynbee frequently pays tribute to the importance of his work at Chatham House in terms of its contribution to *A Study*.

He feels he could have done neither *A Study* nor the *Survey of International Affairs* if he "had not been doing the other at the same time." A study of current events needs the background of world history; "and a study of world history would have no life in it if it left out the history of the writer's own lifetime." He would have present-day historians study Gandhi, Lenin, Ataturk, and F.D.R. "if he is to have any hope of bringing Hammurabi, and Ikhnaton and Amos and Buddha back to life for himself and for his readers." As Toynbee puts it: "One's contemporaries are the only people whom one can ever catch alive."[40]

As we come to the end of this section, it must seem to many, as it seems to me, that Toynbee was motivated to write *A Study* for noble and worthy reasons. Perhaps some of us would be happier if history and theology had run somewhat more disparate paths. Perhaps his universalistic bias will prove annoying to some.

At times, for me, Toynbee becomes too Anglican and too British. He does not quite rise to that lofty pedestal which would seemingly be a prerequisite for composing universal history. Still, what dare one expect? Wondrously erudite, wondrously imaginative, Toynbee is just one man. "We may remind ourselves," he declares, "of the axiom which we have taken as the starting-point of our present *Study of History*: the axiom that all historical thought is inevitably relative to the particular circumstances of the thinker's own time and place. This is the law of Human Nature from which no human genius can be exempt."[41] This passage is suggestive of one of Toynbee's more generous remarks on the discipline of history. He is discussing the gamut of devices historians have used and are now using. Each one of these may be thought of as a key to unlock doors. He would have us keep each key, even if it unlocks but a single door:

But there did not seem to be any master key that rendered all its fellow keys superfluous by unlocking all doors alike; and therefore a resourceful researcher who had moved by curiosity to explore the wonderland of History would keep on adding to the bunch of keys on his keyring. Whenever he ran into a closed door barring the way to further progress in his intellectual quest, his first recourse would be to try whether any of the keys already on his ring would turn the next door's lock; but, if none of them proved to fit, he would neither try to force the door nor despair of succeeding in opening it, but would set about casting a new key to fit a lock that had been proved by experience to be one of novel structure.[42]

Toynbee graciously gives up some of his keys as he makes his way through the first ten volumes and again in that final volume *Reconsiderations*. Some of his keys are for doors we have neither the heart nor the will to open. I suspect a few are for doors which simply do not exist except in the mind of the keyring owner. Toynbee has been a diligent locksmith; perhaps we can even admire the beauty of the keys that do not work.

II

What is the story Toynbee tells in *A Study of History?* For one thing, Toynbee is not the conventional fare for Americans. He is a system builder. Max Lerner, among others, has told us that Americans are not given to this sort of thing.

Americans, whether in political science, economics, culture, nature, or God, have very little "grand theory" according to Lerner. Even when one turns to some of America's most eminent thinkers, what one gets is "a rich array of fragments rather than an artfully laid out master plan." All of this is in sharp contrast to European thought.[43]

We seem not to be tuned to grand theory, and Toynbee is if anything the grand theorist, perhaps the grandest theorist of them all. It is just possible that he himself gets lost every now and then in his process of lofty theorizing. *A Study of History* is big enough to lose both its author and its readers. But let us try to construct a few signposts.

For six huge volumes Toynbee is preoccupied with the concept of civilization as an intelligible unit for historical study. He early arrives at the conviction that nothing smaller than a civilization can be an intelligible unit.

Civilizations pass through four stages: the age of growth, the time of trouble, the universal state, and the interregnum, or the stage of disintegration. Other systematizers have also discussed historical stages. Spengler's organic stages are spring, summer, fall, and winter. Comte's philosophical pattern is composed of theology, metaphysics, and positive science.

1. The age of growth. This story revolves largely around Toynbee's idea of challenge-and-response. In order for a civilization to grow and prosper it must be challenged. If the challenge is excessive, the civilization will withdraw in one way or another. For example, the Eskimo faced an excessive challenge from the severe climate. By a *tour de force* he survived, but he did not progress. Similarly, the nomad in the desert faced an excessive challenge. His response was to take to the horse and wander about without ever setting up a permanent seat of government. "Civilizations grow," according to Toynbee, "through an *elan* that carries them from challenge through response to further challenge and from differentiation through integration to differentiation again."[44]

Superficial criteria for this stage include increasing command over the human environment—a sound economic, military, and political organization, as well as increasing control over the physical environment—dams, roads, and a food supply. More basically, the period of growth is best described as "progress towards self-determination." The challenge arises increasingly from within the culture and less and less from the outside: "Growth means that the growing personality or civilization tends to become its own environment and its own challenger and its own field of action."[45] We seem once again brought around to the Socratic maxim know thyself:

It is through the inward development of personality that individual human beings are able to perform those creative acts, in their outward fields of action, that cause the growth of human societies; and so we find that this enhancement of the individual's mastery over the Macrocosm is the consequence of a corresponding achievement in the Microcosm—of a progress in self-articulation or self-determination within. The outward and the inward advance in organization and increase in power are so intimately connected that either can be described in terms of the other.[46]

Progress is ever upward; there is no rest, no stopping. To do so is to regress: "The climber has not yet reached the ledge above him where he may hope to find rest . . . for unless he continues to climb on upward until he reaches the next ledge, he is doomed to fall to his death."[47] We are thus forever under challenge. In a growing state we make a "response which not only answers the particular challenge that has evoked it but also exposes the respondent to a fresh challenge which demands a fresh response on his part."[48]

During the age of growth we have such rhythms as Yin and Yang, expansion and contraction, withdrawal and return, challenge and response. Each return, each successful response, makes for ever greater self-determination in a civilization.

2. Time of troubles or breakdown. Toynbee does not accept Spengler's organic account of civilization: "To declare dogmatically that every society has a predestined time-span is as foolish as it would be to declare that every play that is written and produced is bound to consist of just so many acts."[49] In one paragraph Toynbee sweeps away a host of theories, namely, that civilizations run down as the clockwork of the physical universe; that civilizations are like living organisms with a fixed life cycle and life span; and that the breakdown of a civilization may be ascribed to the racial degeneration of a given people.[50]

Nor will Toynbee have anything to do with Gibbon's barbarian invasion explanation. Civilizations die of suicide, not by murder. These so-called barbarians are just plunging their swords into "the body of a suicide whose life-blood was already ebbing away through a self-inflicted wound." The barbarian gives "the expiring suicide his *coup de grace* or he devours his carcass after it has already become carrion":[51]

Our inquiry into the causes of the breakdowns of civilizations has led us, so far, to a succession of negative conclusions. We have found that these breakdowns are not acts of God. They are neither the inexorable operations of a Saeva Necessitas nor the sadistic sport of a Kali snatching another bead for her necklace of skulls. Nor are they the vain repetitions of senseless laws of Nature, like monotonous revolutions of the Earth around its own axis and of the planets around the Sun, or like the mechanical churning of the arms of the windmill which lifted Don Quixote out of his saddle . . . we cannot legitimately attribute these break-downs to a loss of command over the environment, either physical or human. The breakdowns of civilizations are not catastrophes of the same order as famines and floods and tornadoes and fires and shipwrecks and railway accidents; they are not the equivalent of mortal injuries inflicted in homicidal assaults.[52]

The breakdowns occur from a loss of self-determination just as "progress towards self-determination is the criterion of growth." They result from a failure in creativity, from an idolization of an outworn technique or institution that has been effective for one challenge but not for the next one. The idolization may fix itself on slavery, a form of government, or a particular type of marketing. A society may disintegrate because it adopts a "time-machine" with which to escape into a future or with which to bury itself in a past.

3. Universal states. During the time of troubles there are petty clashes; wars break out all over the place. A universal state is established to put down these wars, to bring unity to the warring classes within the state. Pax Romana is established. The universal state appears to be a blessing. There is peace which is welcomed after all the recent strife. Prosperity is likely to be the condition of society, but civilization is resting on its oars and growth has come to a stop. Universal states (1) arise after and not before the breakdowns of civilizations; (2) are the work of dominant minorities who no longer possess creative energies; and (3) are not summers but "Indian Summers, masking autumn and presaging winter."

The goal of universal states is conservation. They represent a holding action. They are an effort to peg a given civilization at its present stage of development. They are not a response to a challenge that will produce a continuity of challenges and responses. This promised land is just a prelude to disaster. Toynbee warns us that the "attempt to secure immortality in this world is a vain effort," and that this is true for both individuals and societies.[53]

The universal state performs important services for men by providing a universal language, roads and canals, a monetary system, a postal system, military protection, etc. "A universal state is imposed by its founders, and accepted by its subjects, as a panacea for the ills of a Time of Troubles. In psychological terms it is an institution for establishing and maintaining concord," declares Toynbee.[54]

The universal state looks good; it is a relief from the time of troubles. But we must remember it is an Indian Summer with winter just around the corner. Universal states tend "to behave as though they were ends in themselves, whereas in truth they represent a phase in the process of social disintegration." A universal state, however long it may last, "always proves to have been the last phase of a society before its extinction."[55] Universal states die hard:

. . .the cyclic rhythm of Rout-and-Rally in which the dominant tendency towards disintegration has fought out its long battles has been apt . . . to take a run of three-and-a-half beats—rout-rally-relapse-rally-relapse—in accomplishing the historical journey from the breakdown of a civilization to its final unretrieved dissolution. . . . This third rally, however, is the last that the disintegrating Civilization finds the strength to make. When, thereafter, the universal state is smitten by a second paralytic stroke, this is the end, not only of this oecumenical body politic, but also of the body social whose life the universal state has prolonged by incapsulating it in a carapace.[56]

They die hard, but once they arrive at this stage, there seems to be no hope. Toynbee keeps hinting that the West may already be at this point in the process.

4. The interregnum—the end. This is the stage at which civilization dies. It is the Spenglerian winter. Out of the universal state, which can afford to be tolerant—being big and strong it is sure of itself—come universal churches which are the work of creative minorities, also known as the internal proletariat.

III

The histories of some twenty civilizations—which are followed through their genesis, time of troubles, universal state, and death—are one phase of the story Toynbee tells in *A Study of History*. This is what the reader finds in the first six volumes. Volume one was begun in 1927, and volume six was published in 1939. Seven years passed—the war years—before Toynbee returned to his work on *A Study*. He had saved his notes for these later volumes; otherwise, he might have found it beyond his power to pick up where he left off.

Somewhat over halfway into volume seven Toynbee makes his great reverse. With scarcely a word of warning, he shocks the reader by telling him that the concept of civilization has proved inadequate and cannot serve as an intelligible unit in history:

> In our inquiry into the relation between churches and civilizations up to this point, we have tacitly worked on the assumption that in the interplay between societies of these two species the civilizations had been the protagonists and that the role of the churches, whether usefully subsidiary or obnoxiously corrosive, had, on either interpretation, been secondary and subordinate. Now that our operations on these lines have proved fruitless, let us try the effect of reversing our point of view. Let us open our minds to the possibility that the churches might be the protagonists and that vice versa the histories of the civilizations might have been envisaged and interpreted in terms, not of their own destinies, but of their effect on the history of Religion.[57]

According to Toynbee the beginnings of a higher religion are derived from primary civilizations through their internal proletariats; true higher religions are derived from secondary civilizations through their internal proletariats. Tertiary civilizations come about through churches acting as a chrysalis. And the internal proletariat of the decaying tertiary civilizations produces a new religion.

From this point on, religion becomes the key concept in *A Study*. Universal states eventuate in universal churches, and the end product of the civilization process is a higher religion.

This process is cyclic, but as in the case of a wheel, as it goes around it makes progress; in the case of a civilization the progress is toward its higher destination:

> On this showing, the successive rises and falls of the primary and the secondary civilizations are an example of a rhythm . . . in which the successive revolutions of a wheel carry a vehicle, not on a repetitive course that the revolving wheel itself describes, but in a progressive movement towards a goal. . . . the wheel of civilization should be the sovereign means of carrying the chariot of Religion forward and upward.[58]

In this new perspective, Toynbee sees Christianity as "the climax of a continuous upward movement of spiritual progress which had not merely survived successive secular catastrophes but had drawn from them its cumulative inspiration. . . . the history of religion appears to be unitary and progressive by contrast with the multiplicity and repetitiveness of the histories of civilizations."[59]

From this point on, history, as written by Toynbee, grows in-

creasingly theological. *A Study* becomes God-centered both in its
descriptive and narrative aspects and in its philosophic and his-
toriographic aspects. Volume ten, which concludes the formal presentation, is entirely devoted to God and Toynbee's acknowledgements to those who have helped him along the long long
way of *A Study*.

Toynbee begins volume ten with the following question: Why
do people study history? He replies, "Every historian will have
his own answer to this question, because he will be speaking
from his own experience." A second question follows: What do
we mean by history? For Toynbee, history becomes a "vision of
God revealing Himself in action." History becomes "a vision of
God's creation on the move."[60] The quest for historical meaning
becomes "ultimately a quest for a vision of God at work in
History."[61] Human affairs are no longer an intelligible field of
study unless they are understood in terms of Toynbee's conclusion that "Man's *Oikoumene*" is a "fragment of God's Universe."

We have now come to Toynbee's City of God. It is largely,
though by no means exclusively, a Christian City of God. And as
we follow Toynbee in his most recent books, this city seems to
grow ever less Christian and, indeed, less and less a City of God.
But that is a story for another time. As an historiographer in the
large sense, Toynbee would have us believe Christianity is the
culmination of other higher religions. Since civilizations come and
go, we may have a religion which "mounts towards Heaven" by
the periodic "downfalls of civilizations on Earth." The movement
of civilizations is cyclic and recurrent, whereas religion moves on
a "single continuous upward line."[62]

IV

Another story to be found in *A Study* is that of the numerous
cycles dear to the heart of Arnold Toynbee. Sometimes the cycle is
no more than the simple night-and-day cycle; at other times it is
that of the seasons or some vast climatological routine covering
periods of five or six hundred years. One cycle deals with the
nomads breaking forth from their plains.

Toynbee asserts that the Nomad eruptions of "maximum effer-
vescence occur at regular intervals of six hundred years."[63] So
once more we see Toynbee finding a pattern which others have

not noted—or having noted it, attach no particular significance to it.

This rhythm and all the various other rhythms make men free, not slaves, says Toynbee. "If human history repeats itself, it does so in accordance with the general rhythm of the universe," and this more universal rhythm allows creation "to go forward" and to reveal itself as an "Instrument for freedom of creative action."[64]

One is sorely tempted to conclude that Arnold Toynbee goes hunting for evidence of God and rhythm in every crook and corner of history and of the universe and that he comes back from each of these safaris with the limit.

V

Toynbee resists encompassment and summarization. Efforts in this direction are self-defeating and frustrating. I suspect this is why some persons dismiss him so perfunctorily. We are exploring the labyrinth of one of the intellectual wonders of the world. It is easy to get lost in this maze and yet in each dead end find oneself confronted with lovely tapestries. But one does grow weary, weary of the endless footnotes and never-ending annexes. There are obvious errors and obvious omissions which encourage facile remarks, like "to hell with Toynbee," and a deep sigh of relief that now with Toynbee out of the way one can get back to the real business of life, however unreal or however unbusinesslike.

Historians have damned Toynbee up one side and down the other. He has been called "no historian." An important aspect of any work of art or letters is how well has the artist or author accomplished his own declared goals. We may ask, therefore, whether Toynbee has succeeded in doing what he set out to do? How does he measure up to his own goals? The answers are obviously related to some of Toynbee's tenets as a historian.

1. History should stress pattern. "The truth which confounds an honestly consistent sceptic is that the human Intellect is so constituted as to be intrinsically incapable of ever thinking about anything at all except in terms of uniformities, recurrences, regularities, laws, rhythms, plots, and patterns of other kinds."[65] The fundamental faith of Western man has been his "belief that the Universe was subject to Law and was not given over to chaos."

2. History should be imaginative. It is not the fraud that Plato

pictures it to be in the *Republic,* not a professional trick. ". . .it
is no exaggeration to say that a constant use of the imagination is
one of the primary necessities for the Human Race."[66]

3. History is curiosity. Passive receptivity is never enough for
the historian. History begins when we have a "mutation of receptivity into curiosity." Without this "creative stirring of curiosity"
our histories would be no more than an "eloquent dumb-show to
no effect."[67]

4. History is feeling as well as intellect. "The Intellect, however, is only one faculty of the Soul. When we think about something, we are apt to have feelings about it, and our impulse to
express our feelings is still stronger than our impulse to express
our thoughts."[68] Feelings about history have produced history
quite as often as thoughts about it.

In *Acquaintances* he claims that the Webbs erred in their work
on Soviet communism because of their proneness "to push their
pursuit of 'objectivity' beyond the point of diminishing returns
and their mistaken assumption that, in the study of human affairs,
one needs to discount the human factor if one is to get at the
realities."[69] He has something to say about objectivity and the
Nazi: "A flat-faced account of the Nazi atrocities would be out of
touch with reality."[70]

5. History is contemporary. "Alfred Zimmern taught me that
all 'true history is contemporary history.' "[71] As Toynbee listened
to Sir Alfred, partitions between past and present, between ancient and modern, disappeared.

6. History is partly myth. "In Mythology, the distinction between facts and fictions is left undrawn; and while History has dif-
ferentiated itself from Mythology . . . it has never succeeded in
dispensing with fictitious elements altogether."[72] We cannot get
along in history without mythological elements.

7. There is nothing wrong with mixing theology with history.
In *Civilization on Trial,* Toynbee has an essay entitled "The
Meaning of History for the Soul." He writes that he ventures into
the field of the soul "in the hope that it may be of some interest
to theologians to see how these old theological questions are ap-
proached by a historian."[73] Much of *A Study* is more theological
than historical. His book *An Historian's Approach to Religion,*
published in 1956, is clear evidence of his interest in theological
matters.

8. Toynbee believes in historical prophecy. To the question

what will the historian say in 2047? he answers, "The great event of the twentieth century was the impact of Western civilization upon all the other living societies of that day." And he prophesies that by the year 3047 Western civilization will have been transformed "by a counter-radiation of influences from foreign worlds which we, in our day, are in the act of engulfing in ours."[74] By 4047 the historian will be discussing developments which led up to the unification of man. By then, the parochial heritage will have been "battered to bits by the collision with other parochial heritages," and from this wreckage a new common life will emerge.

Finally, in the year 5047 the historian will be saying that "the importance of this social unification of mankind was not to be found in the field of technics and economics, not in the field of war and politics, but in the field of religion."[75]

Why does Toynbee engage prophecy? For one thing, we have some 6,000 years of past history to help us to extrapolate into the future. There is a kind of balance: the further back in time our history goes, the more distant into the future our prophecies may extend.[76] And he does it because it is his belief that the historian should always seek to know how this came out of that, how this turns into that.

9. He loves the long view. I would suspect that he is quite fond of the following quotation from Berdyaev: "History is the result of a deep interaction between Eternity and Time; it is the incessant eruption of Eternity into Time."[77]

10. He is committed to the universal view of history. He would see all and somehow bring it all into a meaningful unity. Universality is an insistent and recurring theme in *A Study;* and in *Reconsiderations*, he is still on this theme: "There is no escape from the formidable requirement that we must each of us attempt to take a panoramic view of the whole field."[78]

11. He candidly admits his own feeble perceptive powers. He realizes that he has but a "fleeting and fragmentary vision of the passing scene. He admits that "the only light we can throw on the past is the light of our own experience." Each historian works "in a particular social milieu at a particular stage in its development."[79] Each will have his particular pair of spectacles, his particular blinders.

Many historians have declared Toynbee a failure. But if the criteria given above are even in a small way an accurate picture of what Toynbee would like to achieve as an historian, then I think we have no choice but to say that Toynbee's *Study of History* is a noble work admirably executed. We will have to admit that Toynbee accomplished what he started out to do. If we would judge him harshly, then we shall have to do this with evaluative criteria other than Toynbee's own.

And let us add before we get red in the face with anger or simple frustration at this embalmer of civilizations—this historian turned theologian—that Toynbee himself has reminded us that *A Study of History* is not history; it is a study of history only in the same manner that a study of Dante is not Dante. However, the difference in the case of Dante seems more self-evident. In a fundamental sense, I fear we can rarely, perhaps never, find Toynbee self-evident.

CHAPTER 2

The West as Hubris

In seeking new beginnings, men are now haunted by an image of the end of everything

Robert Jay Lifton in
History and Human Survival

T WO historians stand out preeminently as being haunted by an image of the end of everything or, if not the end of everything, then at least the end of the West. These two are Oswald Spengler and Arnold Toynbee. One may take a certain perverse comfort in knowing that if the West is to go under, it will have had the pleasure of reading its own obituary, the most erudite and voluminous obituary ever penned. And no Westerner can protest that he was not warned.

I

Both men are bold. Toynbee speaks of a "deep impulse to envisage and comprehend the whole." Spengler speaks of his goal as that of formulating a "morphology of world history." Of these two historian-eschatologists, the German is the more fatalistic, the less hopeful. The Spenglerian historic table is a good deal simpler than, say, the periodic table for the elements devised by Mendeleev. It is no more than the life cycle of an organism:

Cultures are organisms, and world history is their collective biography. Morphologically, the immense history of the Chinese or of the Classical Culture is the exact equivalent of the petty history of the individual man, or of the animal, or the tree, or the flower. . . . the comparative morphology of plants and animals has long ago given us the methods. . . . Every culture passes through the age-phases of the individual man. Each has its childhood, youth, manhood and old age.[1]

This is not one of a series of possible accounts; this is the necessary, true account. Each of the stages in every culture "has a de-
finite duration, always the same."[2]

Spengler anticipates that such a thesis will not enjoy wide
popularity. It will be objected that such a view which gives "certainty as to the outlines and tendency of the future" will cut off
"all far-reaching hopes" and will be "unhealthy for all and fatal for
many, once it [ceases] to be a mere theory and [is] adopted as a
practical scheme of life by the group of personalities effectively
moulding the future." Spengler makes light of such objections:
"Such is not my opinion. We are civilized, not Gothic or Rococo,
people; we have to reckon with the hard cold facts of a *late* life,
to which the parallel is to be found not in Pericles's Athens but in
Caesar's Rome."[3] Further, he does not see how a vigorous generation with unlimited hopes would deem it a disadvantage that
some of its hopes will come to nothing: "And if the hopes thus
doomed should be those most dear, well, a man who is worth
anything will not be dismayed."[4]

Spengler would have men aware of the dread necessity which
faces them. This awareness is better for men than the optimism
another philosophy of history might encourage. Freedom (a risky
word says Spengler) takes on a different meaning in *The Decline
of the West:* "We have not the freedom to reach to this or to that,
but the freedom to do the necessary or to do nothing."[5] Up to
the present men have been at liberty to have a hopeful view of
the future. Without facts, sentiment takes over, Spengler declares. "But henceforward it will be every man's business to in-
form himself of what *can* happen and therefore of what with the
unalterable necessity of destiny and irrespective of personal
ideals, hopes or desires, *will* happen." He cautions us that the
future of the West is not "a limitless tendency upwards and onwards for all time towards our present ideals."[6]

An historic morphology based on the life cycle of an organism
has to come to terms with death. There is not this eternal upwards and onwards, but rather decline and death. Spengler
seems at times to anticipate aspects of the existentialist mood:

. . .when man first becomes man and realizes his immense loneliness in
the universal, the world-fear reveals itself for the first time as the essentially human fear in the presence of death, the limit of the light-world,
rigid space. Here, too, the higher thought originates as meditation upon

death. Every religion, every scientific investigation, every great symbolism attaches its form-language to the cult of the dead, the form of disposal of the dead, the adornment of the graves of the dead. . . . From this primitive fear springs, too, historical sensitiveness in all its modes.[7]

How does all this Spenglerian talk go down with Toynbee? Not too well it seems. Our Englishman finds his German colleague stating his thesis that cultures (or civilizations) are organisms given "in such uncompromising terms that it virtually refutes itself." He calls Spengler's tendency to personalize civilizations as organisms "a peculiar infirmity."[8] Toynbee finds Spengler's extension of the progress in art to many other phases of human life an example of "magnificent logic" but adds, "Logic or no logic, we cannot follow Spengler as far as this."[9]

Toynbee objects to Spengler's thesis that a civilization is a single block. In the latter, a given civilization is assigned "an absolute and all-pervasive qualitative individuality." This view is unacceptable to Toynbee because he sees a civilization as a process which cannot be evaluated on the basis of a single attribute. There are emergent factors. As we move from primitive to higher civilizations, qualities possessed by an earlier civilization do not persist in the same manner or intensity.

Spengler keeps turning up in *A Study of History*. In volume III, Toynbee complains that a note of "over-emphasis and hyper-dogmatism" is a "serious blemish in Spengler's remarkable work." In volume IV, he refers to the organic theory of history as "the death-sentence demanded by our most celebrated post-war exponent of a philosophy of history."[10] Later, Toynbee writes:

Herr Spengler is demanding from us much more than a recognition of empirically verifiable facts. He is asking us to induce from this handful of facts a universal and inexorable law; and, with (no doubt, unconscious) jugglery, he is attempting to mask the inadequacy of the evidential basis on which his tremendous induction has to stand, behind the simile in which he likens the career of a civilization to the life-history of a human being or other living organisms. As an effective artifice of literary expression, this simile might have been allowed to pass; but, when we detect its author in the act of misusing it for the purpose of glozing over a weakness in his chain of argument, we are bound to point out that this simile has no basis in fact. . . .

We have noted that societies are not, in fact, living organisms in any sense; and that we may be sure that our apparent glimpses of a living and breathing Leviathan will resolve themselves, under cold scrutiny, into the prosaically inanimate realities of a bunch of gasometers or a pall of smoke on the horizon. . . . To declare dogmatically that every society has a predestined Time-span is as foolish as it would be to declare that every play that is written and produced is bound to consist of just so many acts, or that every film that is photographed and thrown upon the screen is bound to measure just so many yards or metres.[11]

The war of words continues into volume IX. This "undocumented Determinism" is an "airy conceit" which Spengler has crystallized into "the ponderous dogma under which a man of genius has perversely buried the brilliant findings of his intuitive insight." Toynbee regrets that his "philosopher-hierophant" has not stated the facts but had to import "the ex cathedra judgment that they are also the fore-ordained acts of an ineluctable Destiny." This determinism represents "the spectacle of Spengler's self-stultification."[12]

If some of this sounds vaguely familiar, it may be that others have viewed Toynbee somewhat as Toynbee views Spengler. It seems to me that it is to Toynbee's credit that he did not search out an analogy as his primary construct for *A Study*. He arrived at his thesis by examining some twenty civilizations and then invented a new set of terms to describe the stages in the process of an advancing civilization. In avoiding an analogy, Toynbee is in accord with Lord Bryce, who maintained that the chief practical use of history is to deliver us from plausible historical analogies.

A man of genius or near genius does not of necessity make his contribution solely on the basis of the amount of truth in his work. On this count, we should have to live with a mere handful of eminent men. Spengler tells us that understanding the world means "being equal to the world." Perhaps Spengler's greatest contribution is that he widens our search for meaning.

Spengler lived at a time when certain prominent men entertained utopian aspirations of progress. Among them we may name Wilson, Lenin, Wells, and Shaw. It was Spengler's *Decline of the West* which most dramatically challenged this Western philosophy of progress. Perhaps the West needed a challenging reminder that it was in a state of decline. Spengler says he hit upon the title in 1912. Five years later, he observed that events had justified much and refuted nothing of his thesis. The optimism of infinite and inevitable progress can be a harmful and misleading doctrine no less than the pessimism of finite and inevitable decline. Spengler moderated the optimism which seemed so much a part of the Western ethos. With him, the prospect of decline became one of the alternative views of the world. In the light of events since World War I, one must conclude that decline is not impossible and that progress is not inevitable. Perhaps now, in retrospect, one may still say that a residual Spenglerian pessimism has done something to make us more equal to the world. This is one uncertain contribution.

Whitehead holds that as we mature intellectually we should shed details for general principles. Goddard and Gibbons hold that Spengler does this for us. While these two men find *Decline of the West* suffering neglect and contempt, they conclude that Spengler's vision will give form and meaning to what would have otherwise been "an incoherent mass of facts and ideas." One can accept this much from Goddard and Gibbons, but when they go on to hold that Spengler's law of civilization may become with some minor modification a law which controls "the periodicity of events and changes,"[13] they are surely going too far. F.C.S. Schiller gives us a likely rebuttal: "The decline and fall of a civilization may always be due to human stupidity and to a reiteration of the same fatal blunders, rather than to the blind necessity of an inexorable law."[14] According to Schiller, no law can provide for or against "the intrusion of real novelties."

Schiller prefers to look upon Spengler's ideas "as interesting suggestions rather than as established dogmas." Each idea may have some merit, he declares: "A multiplicity of predictions will do no harm; even if it is no guarantee of safety, it at least increases the chances of success, and in any case the audacious forecasts of Prometheus, the prophet, will be more valuable than the caution of Epimetheus, the historian, whose wisdom dates from after the event."[15] We may say then, that with Spengler we have one more prediction.

In a day of bureaucracy and emphasis on objectivity, it is possible that the audacious conceitedness and personalism of Spengler must be put down on the credit side of the ledger. "There are no eternal questions," he states, "but only questions arising out of the findings of a particular being and posed by it."[16] Likewise he would say there are no eternal truths. It is the individual thinker who counts, and in Spengler this means Spengler: "It is the mark of the born philosopher that he sees his epoch and his theme with a sure eye. Apart from this, there is nothing of any importance in philosophical production—merely technical knowledge and the industry requisite for the building up of systematic and conceptual subtleties."[17] To him, the greater the man, "the truer his philosophy." But truth does not insure the philosopher a large audience: "Every high creator in Western history has in reality aimed, from first to last, at something which only the few could comprehend."[18]

Spengler does not seem to be in the news much of late. It is not that the theme of decline in the West has been put out of mind. Rather it would seem that authors today do not want to overwhelm their readers with esoterica from Spengler's now somewhat outmoded erudition. The cosmic beat of childhood, youth, manhood, old age, and death strikes us as too facile either to threaten us or to entertain us. Somehow we cannot accept that freedom means to do the necessary or to do nothing.

II

Spengler holds that there are no eternal questions—only questions related to a particular person—and that every philosophy is the expression of its own time and only its own time. While one may assume that Toynbee would not go so far, it is symptomatic that he begins *A Study of History* with a section entitled "The Relativity of Historical Thought." The first words in this immensely long book are from Zenophanes, who said that if horses could draw, "then horses would draw the figures of their Gods like horses." And the same would be true were oxen able to draw. With that we are immediately thrown into one of the major theses of *A Study*, namely, that the West is the joint product of industrialism and democracy.

Since the nineteenth century the West has lived under the dominion of two institutions: industrialism and democracy. These two have come to the fore because "they offered provisional solutions for the chief problems with which the age had been confronted. Their enthronement signified the completion of the age which had sought and found salvation in them."[19]

It is a main contention in *A Study* that an achievement may attain the status of a *tour de force* and as such freeze a given people into a fixed position, as is the case, for example, with the nomad and his horse or the Eskimo and his boat. Further, a given people may so idolize an achievement that it is magnified in importance well beyond its intrinsic merits.

We need not burden ourselves at this stage with the involved metaphors of Toynbee nor with his dialectics of stagnation. Suffice it to say that for Toynbee the essential ingredient in democracy for his historical eschatology is nationalism; and for industrialism the essential ingredient is technology; and these two institutions—nationalism and technology—pose serious threats to the survival of the West.

Repeatedly Toynbee cries out as a prophet from the Old Testament: mankind, give up your national state; the choice is between a universal state and universal genocide. The unifying work "will never be done by the political devotees of the idol of National Sovereignty." The war between nations has replaced the wars of religion and the wars of kings.

The West put a modern, militaristic, Fascist Germany on the scene, says Toynbee: "If a twentieth-century Germany was a monster, by the same token, a twentieth-century Western Civilization was a Frankenstein guilty of having been the author of this German monster's being."[20] In the nuclear age "nationalism is a death-wish."[21] The West has been unable to escape from looking at history "from that old parochial self-centred standpoint." To Toynbee, sin is the posture of self-centeredness, and the West is in this sense the great sinner; nationalism is "the Western ideological disease."

III

Nationalism's twin threat to the West is technology. This threat has been spelled out perhaps most dramatically by Jacques Ellul in *The Technological Society*. In Ellul, the threat seems to bear down on individual men; in Toynbee, it seems to bear down on whole peoples. In fact, technology threatens nationalism itself. "Western nationalism is a divisive force; Western technology is a unifying force; these two Western gifts are proving incompatible with each other; and, since it is certain that modern technology is not going to be renounced either by the West itself or by its non-Western proselytes, we can predict that Western nationalism is going to the wall," declares Toynbee.[22] This is the optimistic observation on technology.

Technology has given man nuclear fire power which may destroy him. Technology has allowed Western man an arrogance that weakens his chance of ever being able to treat "natives" with genuine respect as an equal.

Industrial productivity by its very nature has stressed the relation of man with his physical environment. This emphasis has had the effect of making for neglect of the relations between man and man in the course of which we have failed "to improve the wisdom or the virtue of the human beings" who now possess such vast technical powers.[23]

We have a "penchant for machinery. . . . This is our Western bent."[24]

In many senses, volume IX is the concluding volume of *A Study*, because volume X is given over to thanks and acknowledgements, volume XI is all maps, and volume XII is Toynbee's confrontation with his critics. The following quotation concludes volume IX.

. . .that progress in Technology, so far from being a guarantee of progress in virtue and happiness, was a challenge to it. Each time that Man increased the potency of his material tools, he was increasing the gravity of the moral consequences of his acts and was thereby raising the minimum standard of the goodness required of him if his growing power was not to turn to his destruction; and, while it was true that, in so far as a human soul succeeded in meeting Technology's spiritual challenge, technological progress might be credited with having been at least the blind and unintentional stimulus of this spiritual achievement, it was also true that each individual soul had to fight the same ever-recurring spiritual battle for itself under a mounting pressure from a Technology whose collective and therefore cumulative progress was bearing down harder on each individual human spirit. In the intolerably mechanized "Brave New World'" conjured into existence by the Western Civilization in its post-Modern age it was hard indeed for any human soul to resist the temptation of becoming a fiend without succumbing to the opposite temptation of becoming a robot. This was the Human Race's predicament as twentieth-century Western eyes saw it, and from this observation no facilely pleasing conclusion could be drawn.[25]

Robot or fiend—these are the unpleasant concluding thoughts after nine long laborious volumes.

Others have seen the postmodern age eventuating in less despairing terms than Toynbee's robot or fiend. For example, Robert Jay Lifton finds contemporary society precipitating onto the scene the protean man—the man who changes his visage readily, who readily takes up various roles. Technology may be seen as instrumental in the two forces which have brought protean man to the fore. Modern man has experienced a "historical dislocation." We no longer sense a cultural connection with our tradition. A second factor is the "flooding of imagery" as a result of our mass-communications networks.[26] If we could only be sure that our typical man would be a protean man and not a robot or a fiend, perhaps we could sleep better.

IV

The West has had arrogance in its technology, and in its religion. These two have long been the twin exports of the West. The Westerner has gone about the globe in the assurance that he belonged to the chosen people of God. Toynbee traces the West's arrogance back to the Jewish idea of a chosen people. Out of religion have emerged two of the West's major sins: class and slavery.

What is more, the West has committed major atrocities: the Crusades, the Spanish Inquisition, the Spanish conquest of Peru, the wars of religion, the slave trade, slavery in the deep South, racial discrimination in Kenya, Central Africa, and South Africa, two world wars, the genocide of the Jews by the Nazis, and the French colonial war in Algeria.

V

Because of the outrages listed above we should not be surprised when Toynbee calls the West "the arch-aggressor" in the world. The West as aggressor is a theme woven into *A Study* and the subject of his BBC Reith Lectures of 1952 published under the title *The World and the West*. I confess that I find Toynbee convincing on this theme. "It has not been the West that has been hit by the world," he declares; "it is the world that has been hit—and hit hard—by the West."[27] He asks his reader "to slip out of his native Western skin and look at the encounter between the world and the West through the eyes of the great non-Western majority of mankind."[28] From all corners of the globe the answer comes back: the West has been the arch-aggressor of modern times. Each people has its own experience of aggression to hold against the West.

The Russian experience is easily tabulated. It is the history most of us know, but we rarely put it together as representative of Western aggression. In 1610, Russia was invaded by a Polish army; in 1709, by a Swedish army; in 1812, by the French; in 1915, by a German army followed by an English-American army; and in 1941 by the Germans.

Turkey and Islam were defeated by the West, and then Turkey under the leadership of Kemal Ataturk was Westernized. China and Japan have been overrun, conquered; and in the present period Japan has been thoroughly Westernized. The "more tolerant philosophical traditions of Confucianism and Buddhism" were challenged by "the religious fanaticism" of Christianity.[29]

In India, the results were and are more extreme:

In India's encounter with the West there has been one experience that has not been shared with India by any other society in the world, India is a whole world in herself; she is a society of the same magnitude as our Western society; and she is the one great non-Western society that has been, not merely attacked and hit, but overrun and conquered outright by Western arms, and not merely conquered by Western arms but ruled after that, by Western administrators. . . . India's experience of the West has thus been more painful and more humiliating than China's or Turkey's.[30]

In more general terms, Toynbee comments that contact with the West has given non-Western countries an increase in food production through irrigation and new crops. Yet in every case this increase in food has not been used to improve the standard of living of a stationary population, "but in maintaining the largest possible population on the old level, which was and is only just above the starvation level."[31]

But we have by no means concluded our inventory of the aggressions of the West upon the world. The Africans "were enslaved and deported to minister to their Western masters' greed for wealth." The American Indians "were swept aside." The story is everywhere the same: the West is the arch-aggressor of modern times: "This indictment will surprise, shock, grieve, and perhaps even outrage most Westerners today." But this judgment seems a sound one for the past four and a half centuries.[32]

More than once Toynbee remarks that he fears the price the West will have to pay for its treatment of China. We can already see the non-West awakening as a sleeping giant. Frantz Fanon writes: "decolonization is always a violent phenomenon," "a program of complete disorder."[33] And Sartre has warned:

Make no mistake about it; by this mad fury, by this bitterness and spleen, by the permanent tensing of powerful muscles which are now afraid to relax, they have become men: men because of the settler, who wants to make beasts of burden of them—because of him, and against him. Hatred, blind hatred which is as yet an abstraction, is their only wealth.[34]

It was the Westerner who coined the word "native." Few have given a more incisive elaboration of the meaning of native than Toynbee:

The decisive downward step . . . is not the change "Unbeliever" to "Barbarian", but the change from "Unbeliever" to "Native", in the definition of the stigma by means of which the oppressor seeks to rob his victim of an inalienable humanity. In stigmatizing the members of an alien society as "Natives" of their homes, "top-dog" is denying their humanity by asserting their political and economic nullity. . . . By designating them as "Natives", he is implicitly assimilating them into the non-human fauna and flora of a virgin "New World" that has been waiting for its predatory and acquisitive latest human discoverers to enter in and take possession in virtue of a right of "eminent domain" over a "Promised Land" deemed to be the gift of some war-goddess of Private Enterprise.[35]

The top dog can clear them from the land, drive them on or kill them or keep them to serve as a kind of "efficient human sheepdog." But today "the native's muscles are always tensed."[36]

The West has now "swallowed" at least eight alien civilizations and possibly ten, according to Toynbee. By the 1960's and 1970's, this diet was proving too much for the settler. Europe, which was once a center from which "energy and initiative radiate outwards," has become a center on which non-European energy and initiative converge. Russia and China continue to invade the West with their Marxist philosophy and revolution. Algeria has left its mark. Toynbee's 1954 remarks on Indochina may be seen as a prophecy fulfilled:

An observer of human affairs in the twentieth century of the Christian Era could not look around him without perceiving that the malaise that met his eyes everywhere had been produced by the radiation of Modern

Western economic techniques as well as Modern Western political institutions. The demoralizing effect of an imported Western Industrialism was particularly conspicuous in South-East Asia, where an exotic industrial revolution, speeded-up by the forced draught of importunate Western economic enterprise, had produced a geographical mixture of socially still unannealed communities in the process of gathering the human fuel for its economic furnace.[37]

Toynbee quotes J. S. Furnivall to the effect that what Western efficiency had done was to build a monumental Western skyscraper on Eastern soil while leaving the natives in the basement.[38] One wonders what Toynbee would have to say on seeing the Americanized Saigon in the 1970's.

To a non-Westerner, it must seem as though the Western robot and the Western fiend became one in Indochina with the planes and the napalm. There we can sense that the native's muscles are tensed. The colonial's homeland drags on in protest, politics, racism, and traffic jams. The Western heart grows weary in the face of tensed muscles. The Western soul is less sure of itself: maybe there are no chosen people.

VI

Robert Jay Lifton has introduced the concept of immortality as an historical concept. At first, he claims, immortality was "Magical"; then "supernatural"; and in our day the "symbolic expression of human continuity." This symbolic or revolutionary immortality is the result of man's facing "inevitable biological death." Man now needs a sense of living on after his own death. This is a good deal more than a denial of death; it is an effort of man to bind himself to "significant groups and events removed from him in place and time."[39]

For many, the word *immortality* may carry too heavy a burden of religion, of superstition; however, "human continuity" would likely be an acceptable term for both secular and religious usage. Nuclear warfare threatens this continuity in a way neither wars nor plagues threatened it in the past. We are troubled. According to Ellul, "History is accelerating while at the same time all that could make our presence endure scatters like ashes."[40] Our art works and our ideologies, "though often brilliant or powerful, no longer turn into traditions; like the latest fad in painting, they merely become the fashion of a year, or a month," states Louis Kampf.[41] We use various names to describe these phenomena: the generation gap, generational discontinuity, historical discontinuity, the age of acceleration, *Future Shock*, etc. Lifton says we live, not in an age of anxiety, but rather in an age of psychic numbing. This numbing is our defense mechanism. We cannot physiologically, intellectually, or spiritually react to the multiplicity of events. So we become numbed; and a few achieve a certain charm of nostalgia by writing: "I sometimes think how pleasant the tempo and movement of life was when the speed limit was about eight miles an hour."[42]

We have reason for profound worry about the present and anyone with a decade or two beyond adolescence may find nostalgia irresistible. When the accelerating pace of events snapped historical continuity for Henry Adams around 1900, Adams would counsel: "dispute was idle, discussion was futile, and silence, next to good temper, was the mark of sense."[43]

Toynbee tries to combine good temper with discussion; he will not, even at the age of eighty, imprison himself in either nostalgia or silence. In the face of psychic numbing and the need for immortality symbolic or physiological, he means to take a good look at the West.

Thanks largely to technology, the West is currently ascendant, or, in any case, has enjoyed some years of ascendancy in the twentieth century; "and it looks almost as though a radical Westernization of the entire world were now inevitable," states Toynbee. The West "has expanded to take in the whole of mankind." What we see is an attempt by "Western man to 'westernize' the world," he concludes.[44] The following passage will serve to document the case of the hard time the non-Westerner is having in keeping up: "Technology is perhaps the one product of human activity in which there has been continuous progress, and it has also been a province in which the network of human relations has always embraced the whole human race."[45]

While technology may possess this universality, it remains true, as Toynbee observes, that some peoples may enter a given technic period "as much as ten or twelve thousand years later than the pioneer inventors."

But technological success, however universal, however dominant, cannot be the full story in Toynbee's perspective.

The West's ascendancy is based on technology, and this technology has brought us military technique, which in turn has given us nuclear weapons. However, this ascendancy has a failing for it is difficult to create a technology, but it is easy to acquire a technology from its inventors by borrowing and imitation. As a consequence an ascendancy based on technological superiority cannot be a lasting one.[46] The non-Westerner has been learning the West's technology, and this is modifying the West's ascendancy.

Toynbee speaks of the West's "brief period of ascendancy" and in this way indicates his reservations about the present success and the eventual fate of Westernization. There are already cracks in this dominance which may indicate that the West is in a state of decline.

Toynbee sees a series of challenges being put to the West and a series of weaknesses within. It is his view that civilizations die as suicides and that the external forces only arrive in time to plunge a knife into a putrescent corpse. We have already hinted at some of the internal challenges to the hegemony of the West. There is the Russian challenge, the Western heresy of Marxism.

The West has worshipped false gods, and most of these gods can be subsumed under the heading of technology or science. The West tried to win with technology. But the challenge of communism means that this encounter between the world and the West has "moved off the technological plane on to the spiritual plane." According to Toynbee, success on the technological plane comes easy but not so on the spiritual plane. Man has enjoyed "a dazzling success in the field of intellect and 'know-how' and a dismal failure in things of the spirit." This failure is unfortunate, Toynbee declares, "for the spiritual side of man's life is of vastly greater importance for man's well-being."[47] Once Toynbee has come to the conclusion that the West is a spiritual failure, its future must be at best uncertain.

But there are still other factors. The West is self-centered—a major sin in the Toynbeean context. The West has to be constantly reminded that it has "never been all the world that matters." It is not the sole actor on the stage. "There never has been a human personality, community, or society that has not been tempted," states Toynbee, "to commit the fatuous impiety of trying to put itself in the place of its Creator by casting itself for the role of being 'the Chosen People' and 'the Heir of the World.' "

We may note self-idolization most in evidence "not as a self-adjudicated reward for success, but as a self-exculpating compensation for failure."[48]

Two factors stand out in Toynbee's writings as causes for the decline of civilizations: war and class. Whenever we find a civilization either dead or moribund, "we invariably find the cause of death to be either War or Class or some combination of the two."[49] Western man has solved neither. Once a war would not have been such a great catastrophe because all human destinies "had not been gathered into one basket." But today: "A worldwide catastrophe might leave not a single egg unbroken."[50]

Affluence in the West makes for class among individuals and among nations: "affluence brings with it an automatic penalty. It inevitably insulates the rich minority from the poor majority of the human race." Toynbee sees the United States handicapped by affluence and racism. America can lead only if it can throw off these twin handicaps.[51] Toynbee is not optimistic on either count.

And there is that great Western evil of nationalism.

Spengler had a certain Teutonic directness. The West was caught up in this organic cycle: birth to death, spring to winter. Toynbee, too, has his cosmic beat, his periodicity, but the reader will find nothing so simple as Spengler's cycle. Toynbee's periodicity is vastly complex, and he is not above changing his cyclic rhythms from one volume to another. And when we come to the West, we find Toynbee a hesitant periodicist and a reluctant prophet. In volume IV (1939) he states that we cannot tell whether Western civilization "has already broken down or whether it is still in growth."[52] Or again, he suggests that this civilization may "have passed its zenith for all we know."[53] In volume VI we find this delightful metaphor:

The position of our Western Society in our age cannot become known with any certainty of knowledge till the voyage has come to an end; and so long as the ship is underway the crew will have no notion whether she is going to founder in mid-ocean through springing a leak or be sent to the bottom by colliding with another vessel or run ashore on the rocks or glide smoothly into a port of which the crew will never have heard before they wake up one fine day to find their ship at rest in dock there. A sailor at sea cannot tell for which, if for any, of these ends the ship is heading as he watches her making headway during the brief period of his own spell of duty. To plot out her course and write up her log from start to finish is a task that can be performed only by observers who are able to wait until the voyage is over.[54]

A few pages later we read: "We cannot say for certain that our doom is at hand; and yet we have no warrant for assuming that it is not." To make the latter assumption would be to hold that "we are not as other men are."

In volume VII (1954) Toynbee shifts his basic metahistorical concept from civilization to higher religions. This radical restructuring of the historic periodic table may confuse the reader; but Toynbee himself makes the change without breaking stride and comes forth with a prophecy for the West not very different from the prophecies in the previous six volumes: "The symbol which a stricken Twentieth Century sees glimmering through the darkness ahead is not a skull-and-crossbones: it is a question mark."[55] And this question mark shines through the darkness neither with go-ahead green nor stop red "but is cryptically neutral yellow." Toynbee confesses that any assessment of the West's prospects are difficult "because in A.D. 1952 the plot of this Occidental drama had not yet arrived at its denouement."[56]

While Toynbee remains uncertain whether the ship of Western civilization will arrive at port or go down in midsea, he is not above giving advice of how to keep it afloat for some years more. The West has to avoid "self-destruction without falling into self-stultification." The job is to hold to course and "trust in God's grace." This calls for "contrite humility" and an "indominable endurance."[57]

In 1960, Toynbee wrote: "The history of the West is today an unfinished story."[58] But he hazarded that, if the West was not dying, its ascendancy was manifestly passing away because, as we have already noted, this was an ascendancy based on technology.

In 1970, Toynbee sounded an optimistic note—a rather untypically optimistic note for those of us who have come to know Toynbee in A Study. The quality in human nature which allows us to hope is man's "proven adaptability." Man has survived the test of one apocalyptic event after another. He has transformed himself from a nomadic food-gatherer and hunter into a sedentary farmer and livestock shepherd. Man has already survived much, and this is the source of hope that he may survive his present ordeal and future ones.[59] It is the old story: if fathers could do it, then surely sons can do it. Henry Adams put it somewhat differently earlier in the century. From 1200 to 1900 the movement from unity to multiplicity had been continuously accelerating. If prolonged another generation, a new mind would be required. But thus far, says Adams, the mind had responded successfully, "and nothing yet proved that it would fail to react—but it would need to jump."[60]

Today, in an age of nuclear energy and Westernization, it appears that the mind still needs to jump and the heart needs to love. And there would still glow through the darkness that question mark in neutral yellow color.

VII

Most authors are content to display their erudition by means of numerous and sometimes elongated footnotes. Not so Arnold J. Toynbee. The footnote documentation in *A Study of History* could very well be the most extensive and most elaborate in the long history of scholarship. But even this is not enough. Toynbee indulges in appending annexes and annexes which deal with annexes to his chapters, and the reader must imbroil himself in what are really footnotes, although they may run to some thirty to fifty pages, which in turn are generously footnoted.

At no point in *A Study* does Toynbee devote a chapter exclusively to the United States. With his eye at the telescopic lens, the USA fades into a landscape called Western civilization. Yet it would seem an act of inexcusable omission to have given the above discussion of the West without following this up with some examination of what Toynbee has to say about the United States. It is comforting to know that Toynbee takes cognizance of our nation; but what he has to say is on the whole not at all very flattering.

The United States, for whatever reasons, is now the leader in the West, a giant in power, in influence. But, if we may believe Toynbee, rarely has an ascendant power had so many things going against it. Each of our virtues seems to eventuate in a sin; each strength collapses into a liability.

Toynbee likens the United States to a Great Dane: "I once saw a very big dog blunder into a strange house. This huge creature had a warm heart. For him, every human being, known or unknown, whom he met was, ex officio, a friend."[61] The trouble was that this friendly dog with every wag of his friendly tail broke a

piece of furniture. This Great Dane had the built-in handicap of
size, and there just wasn't a thing he could do about how big he
was.

In the same way the United States has offended the world. Our
giant size is always getting us into trouble with people of normal
stature. But size is by no means our only handicap. We are troubled also by affluence and race feelings.

If the United States wants the good will of the third world, it
can gain this by becoming, as it were, one of them. As a would-
be missionary to the rest of the world the United States suffers
from two insulating factors: affluence and race feelings. These are
two handicaps which in combination could lead to the defeat of
the United States. This is the crushing handicap we suffer in our
competition with Russia "for the good will of the majority of the
human race."[62]

It is normal to be poor; it is exceptional to be rich, says Toynbee. "The penalty of affluence is that it cuts one off from the
common lot, common experience, and common fellowship." It
cuts one off from his "human birthright of membership in the
great human family."[63] There is an automatic penalty of insula-
tion: rich from poor. We have this barrier. But the final result
can be even more fatal. Our affluence is pushing us "into becoming the policeman standing guard over vested interests."

This arrogance of power is making the United States oblivious
to history. It is only our fantastic military power and our willingness to use it along with our affluence that has allowed us to defy
world opinion and thus to go into Latin American countries and
into Vietnam, and these factors, too, have influenced our posture
toward China. We have rushed in where European powers fear
to tread. Colonialism might have ended in 1940 if our country
had foregone the colonial game. "In the eyes of a majority of
mankind," declares Toynbee, "the United States in 1968 was in
the act of trying, in her turn, to build up a colonial empire of the
traditional kind."[64]

What brought the United States to this role among nations?
Toynbee gives rather specific answers to this question. For one
thing our casualties in World War II had been light by compari-
son with those of other lands. But further, we were the one nation (along with Israel) with the experience of having a continuous
series of victories in war. "The general lesson is that any country
which has so far been invariably victorious in a series of past wars

is likely to become a menace both to itself and to the rest of the world," judges Toynbee. During his lifetime, Toynbee had seen "this intoxicating experience" become known to Germany, Japan, the United States, and Israel. The series for Germany and Japan have already ended. This means that most countries "have now been shaken out of mankind's traditional acquiescence in war as being a normal and a tolerable institution."[65] Only the United States and Israel enjoy an unbroken series. Our militarism has been a "success story."

"If it is true that an unbroken series of victorious wars makes a nation dangerous to the rest of the world and to itself," then among the 125 states on this planet the United States and Israel must be the most dangerous, Toynbee concludes. He adds that at this moment they are particularly dangerous because each of them is encountering deep frustration.[66] And a frustrated country may take extreme measures in a nuclear age. Victory may have been beyond our reach in Vietnam, and it is hard to allow an end to come to this military "success story," as both Churchill and Nixon have made clear.

At the very time when there is profound frustration over Cuba and Vietnam, the United States, according to Toynbee, seems to wax ever more militaristic: "This American mood has been alarming because, since . . . Pearl Harbor, the United States has swung round from . . . isolationism to . . . world-wide interventionism."[67] Toynbee finds two symptoms characteristic of militarism. One is that the armed forces become "a state within a state." The second is that most of the military personnel are recruited by conscription. The American people are on both counts "a militaristic people in 1968."[68] What is more, the Pentagon has assumed unbelievable control over facets of American life. It has vast power over the economy because it can pass on defense contracts; and "by research grants, the Pentagon has secured a similar hold over the universities." It has a fine budget for public relations purposes too.

We Americans suffer from illusions. We have waged a crusade against a monstrous force known as monolithic communism. "The Americans have mistaken the identity of the adversary they have challenged in Vietnam. Their opponent there has been, not the mythical monster World Communism, but Vietnamese Nationalism," says Toynbee.[69] ". . .America has collided with Vietnamese Nationalism, and the strength of the resistance with which America has met in Vietnam has been a local expression of a general Asian and African determination to get rid, once and for all, of the West's hated ascendancy."[70]

Toynbee refers to the "progressive Germanization of the American people." He finds us in "a dangerous mood" because absolute power corrupts absolutely. We have delighted in our "technological virtuosity." It is Toynbee's belief that we will see "the moral condemnation of the United States by the rest of the world—a condemnation as severe and as universal as the condemnation incurred by Germany under the Nazi regime, by Japan during the years 1931–1945, and by the Soviet Union under Stalin's rule."[71]

Maybe that Great Dane is not such a friendly dog after all.

We are militaristic in a bad sense; and we are antirevolutionary in a bad sense. We are living at a time when for the first time in history "the masses have now become alive to the possibility that their traditional way of life might be changed for the better and that this change might be brought about by their own action."[72] The amenities of civilization can be extended to all men if we do not use "our new material for committing mass-suicide."

America's relationship to this "new world revolution of the peasantry" has not been a very honorable one, says Toynbee. We have turned our back on revolutions: "Today America is no longer the inspirer and leader of World Revolution. . . . By contrast, America is today the leader of a world-wide anti-revolutionary movement in defense of vested interests. She now stands for what Rome stood for."[73] We have given up our historic role of the leader of the depressed majority of mankind. This role has fallen to Russia, as Toynbee evaluated the scene in 1962.

We have twice seen Germany defeated; and if the United States continues to dedicate itself to the cause of wealth, history will similarly "sweep the United States out of the path of its onward march."[74] The grave question is our attitude toward "the movement for social justice." The acid test will come in Latin America, and thus far the response in Cuba, in Guatemala, and in Chile—has been lamentable. But all is not lost; there is still time for America to rejoin her own revolution.

We're that Great Dane; we're affluent and big and powerful; that militaristic people, that military success story; that archconservative, the antirevolutionary. And further, we're that Madison Avenue materialistic people. Toynbee obviously does not care for

Madison Avenue, a curse to the United States and a potential danger to the rest of the world. To him, "one of the most precious of America's lost human freedoms is the freedom from the tyranny of advertising." It is his conclusion that no other country "outside the United States will ever saddle itself with a Madison Avenue or even hanker after this form of psychological slavery."[75] He senses that "the present American standard of living is not admired by mankind at large."

At this point, Toynbee lapses into a familiar theme: the end of human life is spiritual, and thus our Madison Avenue materialism can only subvert man from his spiritual ends. "The true end of Man," claims Toynbee, "is *not* to possess the maximum amount of consumer goods per head."[76]

These various movements in the West and these particular trends in the United States do not afford an exactly heartwarming prospect. Yet Toynbee declares that he is no predestinarian pessimist: "I have always thought that the future was open for every civilization. . . . But I am a pessimist in the sense that I think we can see very clearly the ways in which people did wreck a number of civilizations."[77] Toynbee thinks we will have no trouble in repeating these very same mistakes.

In that open and not so open future, Toynbee sees through "the lethal glare" of nuclear war a China that "might one day make the Soviet Union and the United States huddle together for mutual protection."[78] Through this same glare we can see "that Man's last enemy is, not death, but Man himself. Man is his last enemy, and his worst one."[79]

CHAPTER 3

War: Nemesis of Civilization

Speaking now *ad hominem*, after having survived two world wars and lived to see the invention of the atomic weapon, I have no doubt about the action that the study of international affairs in my lifetime has enjoined upon me. I am speaking now as a human being, a great-grandparent, and a citizen, not as an historian dedicated to the pursuit of objectivity in his professional work. As a human being, I cannot be content to contemplate the World as I find it. My study of the World will have been barren and irresponsible if it has not equipped and spurred me to do what I can—infinitesimal though the effect of my action may be—to help mankind to cure itself of some of the evil that, in my lifetime, I have seen human beings inflict on each other. I must do all that I can to save my grandchildren and great-grandchild from being overtaken by the fate that has criminally cut short the lives of so many of my contemporaries.

Arnold Toynbee in *Experiences.*

E ARLY in 1955 Toynbee was asked a number of leading questions, for example, what are the major problems facing the world today, as you see them? He replied that the number one problem is "staving off a third world war"; number two, "limiting world population"; and number three, on the assumption that we can solve number one and number two, "the revival of religion."[1]

His response was not casual off-the-cuff journalism. The problems of population and war occupy a significant place in *A Study.* The world's teeming peasantry was threatening "to cancel the benefits of technological progress by continuing to raise the numbers of the World's population pari passu with each successive increase in the means of subsistence that Technology might achieve."[2] Toynbee foresees the possibility that governments may have to intervene with population control measures in order to save the world from famine and expansive tendencies that make for war:

In this forecasting a posthumous fulfillment of Malthus's expectations, we should also have to forecast that, by the time at which the disconcerting gap between the World's food supply and the Peasantry's breeding habits would have brought the Peasantry to the verge of famine, some oecumenical authority would have made itself responsible for looking after at least the elementary material needs of the whole living population of the planet.[3]

In this situation, with a world guarantee of food supply, declares Toynbee, "the begetting of children would have ceased to be the private affair of wives and husbands and have become the public concern of a ubiquitous impersonal disciplinary power." This change would impose on mankind one of the most drastic revolutions of history, "for hitherto men and women had not only been at the liberty to beget children at their own discretion but had enjoyed this freedom when they had been destitute of all other rights and assets."[4] If we are to guarantee freedom from want, then the freedom to beget may have to be taken away. A minimal standard of living would require interference in personal liberty.

Regulating the right to beget clashes with the peasant's way of doing things and it runs counter to certain religious dogmas. All the higher religions in the West have accepted the "cult of procreation" to such an extent that any governmental public policy of birth control would clash with deep-seated religious beliefs. In the event of a head-on collision between religion and population control, Toynbee concludes that the church authorities would champion the "peasant's cherished freedom to reproduce his kind." Yet he feels that the churches would recoil from support of unrestricted breeding if it meant that again the evils of War, Pestilence, and Famine should be let "loose upon Mankind."[5]

Toynbee, of course, is not alone in proposing population control on a world-wide basis. Bergson says we have our choice: Venus or Mars. "But one fact is certain: Europe is overpopulated, and the world will soon be in the same condition, and if the self-reproduction of man is not 'rationalized' as his labour is beginning to be, we shall have war. In no other matter is it so dangerous to rely upon instinct."[6] Bergson holds that an international organization concerned with the abolition of war will have to deal with increasing populations, the closing up of markets, and the cutting off of fuel. His conclusion goes: "The gravest of all is over-population."[7] Bertrand Russell finds three conditions preliminary to making ourselves at home in a technological world: world government, approximate economic equality between different parts of the world, and a nearly stationary population.[8] Lewis Mumford comes to the same conclusion: "All the resources of the planet are finite and limited. At some point, as yet indeterminate, world population must be stabilized: possibly, if the higher development of man is fully considered, at a lower number than the present one."[9] Paul R. Ehrlich would no longer accept Mumford's expression "as yet indeterminate."

Thus far, Toynbee's peace lesson seems to read as follows: national sovereignty must go, technology and democracy must evolve toward a universal world state, and, sooner or later, a world union must do something about man's breeding habits. The emphasis is political organization rather than an appeal to an inner moral conversion to peace, or a moral equivalent to war.

Toynbee does not discuss the issue of war in religious terms; instead, he becomes a good secularist. Virtually all problems turn out to be religious problems for Toynbee, but his exhortations for peace are not those either of the pulpit or of a sacred book.

Another aspect of Toynbee's peace program involves taking peace-making away from the victors. The winners are not ready for it, nor are they qualified, he says: "This swift metamorphosis of deft winners of victory into clumsy makers of peace is a tragedy for all concerned." Treaties are by and large pretty impossible things. A war opens up a whole host of new problems and aggravates old ones. Afterwards we find ourselves at the peace table, and all these complex issues must be settled then and there and for all time. "A peace settlement is an almost superhumanly difficult task; the chances of success are slight," Toynbee concludes. "The peace-making of the war-winners is the worst of all the calamities that War inflicts on those who perpetuate it."[10]

The appropriate men are not around. It is the warriors who gather at the close of a war to make the peace terms. The war-maker's virtues are the peace-maker's vices, avers Toynbee: "The task of peace-making demands the intellectual gift of seeing all round a problem, leaving no element out of account, and estimating all the elements in their relative proportions, and the moral gift of an aptitude for cautious conservatism, ripe deliberation, taking long views, and working for distant ends."[11] Treaties are usually so bad that it is difficult to believe that the settlement has not been "malignantly deliberate." But this is not quite fair. The evil which war-winner peace-makers do is a "product not of a brilliant malignity, but of a deadly blindness." These treaty-makers have just emerged from winning a war; hence "the state of mind in which their war-time achievement has left them is the worst possible state for grappling with the utterly different task which is immediately thrust upon their eager hands *ex officio*."[12]

We are left with a "patched-up peace." The usual result of a war is the defeat of the archaggressor. The peace is devised to give the participants a chance to rest from the turmoil of war, rather than to solve long-lasting problems. These problems, writes Toynbee, are shelved rather than solved.[13]

Since the peace-makers and their inept efforts are not much good, what we get is an "abrupt alteration of Total War with Total Peace," and this sort of up-and-down game is playing havoc with the world in the twentieth century:

In the Early Modern Age of Western history the war-ridden society has been affected like a victim of chronic malaria, whose vitality is permanently lowered by his complaint without his life being brought into jeopardy. In the Late Modern Age the Western Society had been relieved of its malaria thanks to gratifying improvement in the day-to-day performance of Western political preventive medicine, but the patient had been made to pay for this rise in his normal level of health by becoming subject to thunderbolt "strokes" which were as predictably sudden as they are lethally violent.[14]

Toynbee's metaphors are not always very helpful. But we could assist the above metaphor of malaria along a bit by suggesting that man in this late period has been upset by wars as short as the six-day war in the Middle East and the ten-years-plus war in Vietnam. One would also wonder whether the situation today can be described as a cycle between total war and total peace. We can be grateful to Toynbee at least for looking at war with the advantage of multiple metaphors as well as with the parading of its manifest dangers.

In dealing with war Toynbee plays two roles: that of historian and that of prophet. The biblical prophets went about crying out Repent. Toynbee with equal fervor calls out Peace. It is an appeal directed to individual men as well as to governments. The appeal is: peace before we suffer the atomic knock-out blow.

However it is not the horrors of atomic war which first motivated Toynbee to wage his campaign against war. His study of past civilizations led him to infer that an "improvement in military technique is usually, if not invariably, the symptom of a decline in civilization."[15] He gives the following illustration:

An Englishman of the generation that has lived through the General War of 1914–18 may remind himself, in this connexion, of an incident which struck him, at the time, as painfully symbolic. As the war, in its ever-increasing intensity, made wider and wider demands upon the lives of the belligerent nations—like some great river that has burst its bounds in flood and is engulfing field after field and sweeping away village after village—a moment came in England when the offices of the Board of Education in Whitehall were commandeered for the use of a new department of the War Office which had been improvised in order to make an intensive study of trench warfare. The ejected Board of Education found asylum in the Victoria and Albert Museum, where it survived on sufferance as though it had been some curious relic of a vanished past. And thus, for several years before the Armistice of the 11th of November, 1918, an education for slaughter was being promoted, in the heart of our Western World, within the walls of a public building which had been erected in order to assist in promoting an education for life. . . . No reader can fail to understand that when the Ministry of Education of a great Western country is given over to the study of the art of war, the improvement in our Western military technique which is purchased at such a price is synonymous with the destruction of our Western Civilization.[16]

Although Toynbee carries on his war against war throughout *A Study*, it is perhaps volume four, which deals with the breakdown of civilizations, that provides the best insight into his views on warfare. This volume relates the progress of war from religious wars to the sport of kings to world wars supported by industrialism and democracy. It is the story of progress from winning wars to total wars with no winners.

The Prussian General Staff was so dazzled by the brilliance of its own success in 1870 that, forty-four years later, it was still unable to think of a European war in terms of any other strategy, with the consequence that in the General War of 1914–18 the Prussian war-machine brought defeat upon Germany and her allies by evoking an unforeseen *riposte* in the shape of a siege on an unprecedented scale. In 1918 the old methods of 1870 were proved, by the sensational collapse of the previously predominant continental European military Power, to be no match for the new methods of trench warfare and economic blockade. And in the year 1938 it was again already certain that the technique which had won the war of 1914–18 would not be the last link in the chain—if Mankind were so perverse as to go on cultivating the Art of War after it attained a degree of deadliness at which any further indulgence in belligerency seemed likely to bring with it the total destruction of Society.[17]

Certainly the experience of World War II bears out what Toynbee has said above. Our further indulgence in belligerency brought an advance in deadliness. War remains a threat to civilization in the sense that it displays a steady advance in deadliness. Toynbee refers to the exploits of men like Attila and Timur as the "crackbrained megalomania" of homocidal madmen.[18] We may be shocked with Timur's massacre of 100,000 prisoners, his burying alive 4,000 Christian soldiers, and his building twenty towers of human skulls; but militarism shows a progress from Timur on. From ancient Egypt on we can see "the whole tragedy of militarism as it has been acted over and over again" by the rulers "of twenty different civilizations down to our own militarists in the Western World today."[19] Toynbee refers to "the suicidalness of Militarism." We seem more civilized in our conduct of war; but perhaps it is just our health habits, our modern dedication to sanitation, which keeps us from building towers of human skulls.

The truth is that even a short period of time in our own century may serve to show that we are in fact far from civilized in our militarism. Our source is Lewis Mumford:

Up to 1942 the American army even boasted of the fact that it practiced only "pinpoint" bombing of selected military targets. But before the war ended, the military forces of the United States had multiplied the weapons of mass extermination and had employed them on an even more devastating scale than the Fascists had done. A single ordinary bomb raid on Tokyo caused 180,000 casualties in a single night. The atom bomb only wrapped up this method of extermination in a neater, and possibly cheaper, package.

Not the least extraordinary fact about the postwar period is that mass extermination has awakened so little moral protest. It is as if the Secretary of Agriculture had authorized the sale of human meat, during the meat shortage, and everyone had accepted cannibalism in daily practice as a clever dodge for reducing the cost of living. It is not the atom bomb, but our willingness to use any instrument of genocide that constitutes the all-enveloping danger. If militant genocide does not turn the planet into an extermination camp, its potentialities for breeding fear and suspicion may turn it into a madhouse, in which the physicians in charge will be as psychotic as the patients.[20]

Mumford holds that "our army equipped itself between 1945 and 1948 to practice extermination rather than war."[21] Mumford has suggested that our moral revulsion over war is in inverse proportion to the number killed. The emotional shock lessens as we advance from submarine attacks with relatively few casualties to the bomb attacks with many casualties.

Robert Jay Lifton takes the position that only by "psychic numbing" could men live through the experience of the atomic bomb attacks on Japan: "Rather than the age of anxiety we could well speak of an Age of Numbing. To put the matter simply, one cannot afford to imagine what really happens at the other end of the weapon."[22] R. D. Laing writes, "Long before a thermonuclear war can come about, we have had to lay waste our own sanity."[23] Laing estimates that we humans have killed in the last fifty years over one million of our own species. We make our adjustments too easily: "The perfectly adjusted bomber pilot may be a greater threat to species survival than the hospitalized schizophrenic deluded that the Bomb is inside him."[24]

Toynbee is far from a psychologist; indeed, there are times when one suspects that Carl Jung is the only psychologist to make an impact on Toynbee. Still he does probe in the direction of psychic matters when he declares that "Militarism is suicidal," and when he declares men must grapple with the question of whether war is intrinsically evil. It is the crucial question on "which the destiny of our civilization hangs."[25] Toynbee felt that the following letter sent him by G. M. Gathorne-Hardy was worthy of inclusion in *A Study:*

"Down to modern time, War was almost universally regarded as something which in itself required no justification. Its drawbacks and horrors were, indeed, recognized, but at worst it was considered an inevitable evil, a calamity, a scourge sent by God, of the same unavoidable nature as the plague. To a community threatened by the Vikings, or other aggressive neighbours, this was the obvious way to regard it. From the victim's point of view there was no distinction in principle between the sudden excursions of such people and those of a horde of locusts or a cloud of disease germs. But this made it all the more natural to admire and honour the prowess of an Alfred or a Charlemagne, who could protect his people from disaster in such circumstances. Down to modern times, though the justification of a particular war might be questioned, and its hardship realized, fighting was all in the day's work, an incident of human existence the abolition of which was hardly an imaginable possibility. In these circumstances, while few may have praised war, everyone valued the warrior, and submitted willingly to his leadership. Down to the nineteenth century the army was regarded as almost the only profession open to a gentleman."[26]

At least we may comfort ourselves by believing that openings for gentlemen are somewhat more varied in our day.

Toynbee is willing to admit military virtues as they were practiced in the past. But as we approach the atomic period he grows less and less willing to say anything good about war.

Volume seven is the first volume of *A Study* to be written in the post–World War II period. More so than in volume four, his comments seem to grow more bitter; there is a new and greater sense of urgency in his remarks on war. He speaks of the threat "to drive a Westernizing World into the supreme public crime and catastrophe of physical self-destruction through a third world war waged with atomic weapons."[27] In volume eight we read:

When Western man had crowned a century of scientific achievement by discovering how to harness atomic energy to the service of War, it looked indeed as if it now lay in his power (if he could reconcile this with his conscience) literally to annihilate the last surviving rearguards of Barbarism in their last remaining pockets of unsubdued territory—always supposing that these condemned barbarian prisoners of a ubiquitous Western Civilization were not reprieved, after all, by seeing the Western masters of the World destroy one another first in an atomic fratricidal warfare.[28]

Toynbee does not lower his voice of war protest as we make our way toward the closing chapters of *A Study*. One war, World War II, had succeeded in reducing the number of major powers from seven to two. What, then, does Toynbee envisage as the result of still another world war? Western science now has up her military sleeve a hydrogen bomb "that could be guaranteed, if ever detonated, to blow even a United States or Soviet Union out of the water—at the cost, perhaps, of making the whole face of the Planet uninhabitable by human or any other living organism."[29] The answer lay in an "oecumenical authority."

As of December 1, 1950, Toynbee held that it was impossible to foresee whether a third world war might engulf mankind in total war. Nor could we be sure that life on this planet would survive such a war now that we had learned to split the atom. [30]

The fate of the world now seemed to fall into two outcomes: either total annihilation or the concentration of power in a single political authority.

Toynbee may disavow accurate prediction, but he does not hesitate to forecast only doom for a world which would go to war now that man has the atomic bomb. There was a time when one could say with some show of cheer and courage: who dies if England lives? "But after Hiroshima the question has been reworded to read: Who can die to make England live, if England has to die with him?" While it may be sweet to die for one's land, it is not so sweet to die with one's land. Under these circumstances, Toynbee wonders whether dying for one's land would be "either gratifying or even meritorious."[31] In Vietnam we have come up with the paradox: to save this city, it must be destroyed.

In *Experiences,* Toynbee expresses his thought that after 1945 the revulsion against war should have become total and universal. In fact, the pre-1914 attitude toward war seems to prevail in all but a few parts of the world. As for himself, he is convinced that if man does not give up war, mankind "is going, sooner or later, to commit mass-suicide."[32]

Toynbee's general disillusionment with warrior virtues seems all but complete: "It looked as if an advancing Western technology's recent success in tapping atomic energy for use in War might have sapped the foundations of a traditional standard of heroism by stultifying some of the most compelling of the traditional motives for it."[33] Four and a half centuries of war in the West had left only two gladiators still erect.

To Toynbee, the outcome of yet another world war would be the imposition of a universal peace, a new Pax Romana, by a victor who had a monopoly of atomic weapons. He is fearful that an atomic war would virtually prohibit any kind of true peace. The spiritual ravages of such warfare would exceed anything we have known, he argues: "Would not the agonies inflicted by atomic warfare make even a once humane and generous-hearted victor turn savage?"[34]

There must be those in the world today who feel that the

United States with an arrogance of power has gone from a humane generous-hearted nation to a savage nation.

The dilemma is an obvious one, declares Toynbee; we need an ecumenical authority. Traditionally the way to arrive at a state of Pax Romana has been war, but we can no longer use this method to achieve peace. However, War can perhaps be avoided, for "if the establishment of a world order [is] imperative for the sake of avoiding an atomic war, the avoidance of an atomic war must be imperative *a fortiori*, and an end in itself."[35] Toynbee is not wholly lacking in optimism on this score. He believes that it is a foregone conclusion that the world is "going to be unified politically in the near future."[36] Our goal is to move from a world of two powers to a single ecumenical power, "and the first concern of the living generation of Mankind [is] that this perilous transit should be accomplished without a third world war."[37]

Perhaps a breathing spell would allow this peaceful transit. What is needed is "time to allow a subconscious Psyche, whose pace was the tortoise's gait, to adjust itself to the revolutionary situation created by the technological conjuring tricks of a Practical Intellect that [has] been racing ahead of its subconscious yoke-fellow at the pace of a march hare."[38] Perhaps we need but look to mankind's right spiritual guides, and Toynbee names Buddha, Jesus, and Francis of Assisi as our right guides, "each of whom scandalized his ascetic-minded contemporaries by the discovery, through personal experience, that love, not asceticism, is the true end of man."[39] So Toynbee wrote in 1970, and we must gather that he will so write until he stops writing. And this may be what he most wants to say when the subject of war comes up.

CHAPTER 4

The Dynamics of Change: Creative Minorities

The whale's belly is simply a womb big enough for an adult. There you are, in the dark, cushioned space that exactly fits you, with yards of blubber between yourself and reality, able to keep up an attitude of the completest indifference, no matter what happens. A storm that would sink all the battleships in the world would hardly reach you as an echo. . . . Short of being dead, it is the final, unsurpassable stage of irresponsibility.

George Orwell in
A Collection of Essays

A S the reader makes his way through A *Study of History* and some half dozen other major volumes of Toynbee, he must from time to time pause to wonder whether he might not be in the belly of a whale. Is A *Study* just so much blubber between the reader and reality? Toynbee is capable of bringing on the nausea of fatigue. However, there is always the prospect that Toynbee can be the source of intellectual excitement, that he can help his reader achieve contact with reality. I feel one of the ways to gain these positive rewards from Toynbee is simply to focus on one of his recurring themes. Reading him seriatim can be overwhelming. One has to zero in on a particular dimension; but even then he seems diffuse.

A major concern of men in the closing decades of our century is social change, historical transition; and this same concern constitutes a major theme in Toynbee. Few men have tried to look at change in such universal terms.

The following quotation impresses me as the most direct and succinct passage in *A Study* dealing with the process of change.

The primitive societies . . . must be actually older than Mankind itself; for, if the prehuman progenitors of the Human Race had not already become social animals, it is hard to imagine how they could have been transfigured into human beings. After Man had become human, he continued to live in primitive societies for hundreds of thousands of years before the first civilizations made their appearance; and the first civilizations were considerably older than the first higher religions. Even the rudiments of higher religions did not appear till some of the civilizations of the first generation were already disintegrating, while the rise of fully-fledged higher religions was subsequent to the breakdown of civilizations of the second generation. Thus our series is a chronological sequence; but it is also a genealogical tree; for the primary civilizations must have been derived from the primitive societies through mutations achieved in response to challenges from the physical environment; the first rudiments of higher religions were derived from the primary civilizations through their internal proletariats; the secondary civilizations were derived from the primary civilizations either through the primary civilizations' dominant minorities or through their external proletariats; the tertiary civilizations were derived from the secondary through higher religions providing chrysalis-churches; and the internal proletariats of disintegrating tertiary civilizations had been creating the rudiments of higher religions of a new generation—rudiments, whose genesis was, at the time of writing, an accomplished fact, though their prospects were still obscure.[1]

Some words of explanation seem in order. There are two dynamics of change mentioned above. We see in one case change being effected by a challenge from the physical environment, such as floods, change of climate, etc. In the second, we see change coming about by means of a minority. Toynbee holds that a physical challenge is the mechanism whereby mankind advanced from a primitive society to a primary civilization. A primary civilization is to be understood as one which is not derived from a previous civilization. It does not have another civilization to serve as a matrix. Once we have arrived at the stage of a primary civilization our mechanism for change becomes that of a minority. The advance from a primary civilization to a secondary civilization, that is, to a derived civilization, is the work of either a dominant minority or an external minority. The mechanism which effects the final change from a secondary civilization to a higher religion is an internal proletariat.

The challenge from the physical environment does not require further elaboration at this stage. Toynbee's thought is that progress at an early stage depends upon some irritation from the environment to keep man on his toes. If the challenge is too severe, man gives up. If it is too weak, he stagnates.

The minority dynamic is more complex and is developed and refined throughout the full length of *A Study*. There are three types of minorities: internal, external, and dominant. Toynbee explains how he uses the word "proletariat." It refers to "any social element or group which in some way is 'in' but not 'of' any given society at any given stage of such society's history."[2] It has no stake in that community.

Toynbee turns to Hellenic culture to illustrate how these three classes operate in a society. The Greeks are the dominant minority, who rule by force because they no longer have any creativeness. They keep order by military force. The Christians are the internal minority or proletariat. In Toynbee, Rome is part of Hellenic culture. The internal minority lives within the geographical area ruled by the dominant minority. They are in but not of Hellenic culture. The barbarians, who live outside the effective control of the dominant minority, are the external proletariat. Rome, the universal state stage of Hellenic civilization, is a locale where the dominant minority maintains itself on the surface; the internal proletariat presses up from below, and the external proletariat brings pressure to bear from the outside.[3] In this situation, hope for the future rests with the internal proletariat:

We have failed to find the immediate object of our search, a permanent and fundamental point of difference between primitive societies and civilizations; but incidentally we have obtained some light on the objective of our present inquiry: the nature of the genesis of civilizations. Starting with the mutation of primitive societies into civilizations, we have found that this consists in a transition from a static condition to a dynamic activity; and we shall find that the same formula holds good for the alternative mode of the emergence of civilizations through the secession of proletariats from the dominant minorities of pre-existent civilizations which have lost their creative power. Such dominant minorities are static by definition; for to say that the creative minority of a civilization in growth has degenerated or atrophied into the dominant minority of a civilization in disintegration is only another way of saying that the society in question has relapsed from a dynamic activity into a static condition. Against this static condition, the secession of a proletariat is a dynamic reaction; and in this light we can see that, in the secession of a proletariat from a dominant minority, a new civilization is generated through the transition of a society from a static condition to a dynamic activity, just as it is in the mutation which produces civilization out of a primitive society. . . . All extant primitive societies must have reached our ledge from an unseen ledge below, and all societies in process of civilization are endeavouring to reach an unseen ledge above; and for all we know, the number of ledges above this and below that may be infinite in both directions. The heights that tower above are quite beyond our powers of estimation, and we have some inkling of the dizzy depths below. . . . We can observe that the alternation between horizontal and perpendicular surfaces on the mountain-side repeats itself in a kind of pattern, and that the corresponding alternation between a static condition and a dynamic activity in the energies of the living creatures that are seeking to scale the mountain similarly recurs in a kind of rhythm. This rhythm has been pointed out by a number of observers living in different ages and different societies, who all agree in regarding it as something fundamental in the nature of the universe.[4]

The process involves three stages: (1) the creative minority degenerates into a dominant minority when it no longer merits the admiration of the members of a given society; (2) as this takes place, the dominant minority resorts to force to maintain its position, and the internal minority secedes without accepting the customs of the dominant ruling class; and (3) this, in effect, brings about a loss of social unity in the civilization and eventuates in the breakdown of that civilization.

These are large brush strokes describing Toynbee's dynamics of change. In his theory of change Toynbee makes much of the Sinitic conception of the Yin and Yang rhythm, which is like the rhythmic movement of the lungs in breathing; Yin and Yang are contraction and expansion, representing a sort of cosmic pulsation which seems to go on beyond any effective control by man.

A less cosmic rhythm, also referred to by Toynbee, is that of withdrawal and return; the action of the internal minority is a withdrawal. Toynbee holds that civilizations "owe their growth to the withdrawal and return of a minority—the Creative Minority which withdraws in order to find a response to some challenge that is confronting the whole society, and then returns in order to persuade an uncreative majority to follow it along the path which it has opened up."[5]

We have in addition to this the withdrawal and return of individuals, who are usually members of an internal proletariat and so have already experienced some of this withdrawal. Withdrawal-and-return is a process which puts much emphasis upon the return. One withdraws in order to return. Withdrawal without return is a selfish, negative act:

We have watched the mystic's soul passing first out of action into ecstasy and then out of ecstasy into action again. . . . The disengagement and withdrawal make it possible for the personality to realize individual potentialities which might have remained in abeyance if the individual in whom they were immanent had not been released for a moment from his social toils and trammels. The withdrawal is an opportunity, and perhaps a necessary condition, for the anchorite's transfiguration; but by the same token, this transfiguration can have no purpose, and perhaps no meaning, except as a prelude to the return. . . . The return is the essence of the whole movement, as well as its final cause.[6]

Toynbee gives numerous examples of this process, beginning with Moses and extending to such things as puberty and penalized minorities: "Yet Yahweh's whole purpose in calling Moses up is to send him down again as the bearer of a new law which Moses is to communicate to the rest of the people."[7] Others mentioned include St. Benedict, the Buddha, Solon, Peter the Great, Lenin, Garibaldi, Kant, and Dante. In the story of Jesus, the withdrawal-and-return motif recurs over and over.

Toynbee returns to this theme in an article entitled "The Desert Hermits" (1970). The citizens of the Roman empire were of the belief that early anchorites and stylites were serving society by leaving it; indeed, it was believed that they were saving it. But they did not return. They remained sitting on their pillars. Those who served or saved were those who returned with a message of love. Toynbee concludes that "mankind's right spiritual guides are not the Christian ascetics but Buddha, Jesus, and Francis of Assisi, each of whom scandalized his ascetic-minded contemporaries by the discovery, through personal experience that love, not asceticism, is the true end of men."[8]

Toynbee is the religious historian, although as a man he may be something yet again. It is religion that moves mankind and history, he declares. Religion is the motive force the internal proletariat provides to a civilization; and over and over religion is the great contribution of individuals who withdraw only to return. The higher religions are "the glorious discovers of the Internal Proletariat."[9] Dominant minorities, on the other hand, characteristically create "schools of philosophy and universal states," and "external proletariats express themselves in barbarian or dissenting religions and in 'heroic' poetry."[10]

The mechanics or the dynamics of change are found in the concepts of challenge-and-response, in withdrawal-and-return, and in the work of dominant, internal, and external minorities. In Toynbee's scheme of things, the internal proletariat, since it gives rise to both the religious leader and the higher religion, is given the key position.

Toynbee is not content to give us just his dynamics of progress; he also gives us his dynamics of stagnation, or perhaps more accurately, his mechanics of stagnation. Civilizations become arrested by attempting and achieving a *tour de force*. A *tour de force* in the Toynbeean context means an adjustment to a severe environmental challenge which freezes a given civilization at a particular stage of development.

They have accepted their challenge as they found it, grasped the projecting rock, and levered themselves over it, outwards and upwards, with a movement of magnificent audacity and vigour and skill. But though the gesture is magnificent, it is not good climbing; for it entails a consequence which the expert climber is ever on the look out to foresee and to avoid. The expert climber is on his guard against making any move that will preclude him from moving on; and our over-audacious climbers cannot break this rule with impunity. . . . Their superabundant skill and vigour and boldness is now all absorbed in a supreme effort to save themselves from falling. . . . They are performing an astonishing acrobatic feat, but a feat in the realm of Statics and not in the realm of Dynamics. In fact, these arrested civilizations, unlike primitive societies, are real instances of "peoples that have no history." Immobility is their unalterable posture, so long as they are what they are. They become what they are by grappling with the projecting crag; they remain what they are by gripping the crag so close that their once free and supple bodies mould themselves stiffly into all the contours of the rock; and they cease to be what they are when they either turn to stone and merge into the crag to which they have clung, or else drop, like a stone, from exhaustion.[11]

Toynbee illustrates this thesis by cultures widely separated in time and space: the Polynesians, the Eskimo, the Nomads, the Osmanlis, and the ancient Spartans. The *tour de force* of the Polynesians was their skill to venture upon long oceanic voyages in their frail canoes; and "their penalty has been to remain in an exact equilibrium with the Pacific." And so they have been frozen, "degenerated into incarnations of the Lotus-Eaters."[12] For the Eskimo, the kayak became the *tour de force;* for the Nomad, it is the horse. The Nomad and the Eskimo have become prisoners of the annual climatic and vegetational cycle. The Osmanlis made their slaves their civil servants: "The Ottoman Padishahs maintained their empire by training slaves as human auxiliaries to assist them in keeping order among their human cattle."[13] Their *tour de force* occurred when they so perfected this system that their slaves became their masters. The *tour de force* of the Spartans was overtraining themselves as warriors.

These dead-end adjustments to the physical environmental challenge lead to two phenomena which retard further progress: caste and specialization. The final result is a regression to an animal form of life.

The Eskimo and the Nomads made their mark by denying their human nature and assuming an animal nature. The Eskimo with his kayak became a seal; the Nomad with his camel became a centaur. They imprisoned their reasoning and their bodies: "They have set their feet on the path of retrogression from humanity toward the animalism out of which Humanity evolved itself once upon a time by one of the greatest creative acts that have yet been achieved in the life-history of the Universe."[14]

Another type of stagnation is the utopia modeled after an insect society. Here Toynbee's thinking bears a good deal of resemblance to that of Karl Popper in *The Open Society and Its Enemies.* In this context, Toynbee, like Popper, has not too much use for those two great Athenians, Plato and Aristotle. The Platonic and Aristotelian political program is to organize an intellectual caste based on the pattern of the Spartan military caste system. In both Plato and Aristotle, "the dry bones of Lycurgean Sparta stick out gauntly through the tender Athenian philosophic skin." Caste and specialization are the results. Plato and Aristotle turn out to be "the docile pupils of the Spartan statesmen of the sixth century."[15]

Toynbee seems quite as opposed to utopias as Karl Popper. A

utopia is simply another *tour de force* which delimits freedom for creative human activity. It is an insect *tour de force:*

> The social insects rose to their present social heights, and came to a permanent standstill at those altitudes, many millions of years before Homo Sapiens began to emerge above the mean level of the rank and file of the Vertebrate Order. And as for the Utopias, they are static not only as a matter of fact but *ex hypothesi*. . . . To arrest a downward movement is the utmost to which a Utopia can aspire, since Utopias seldom begin to be written in any society until after its members have lost the expectation and ambition of making further progress and have been cowed by adversity into being content if they can succeed in holding the ground which has been won for them by their fathers . . . an invincibly stable equilibrium is the supreme social aim.[16]

Stability is the alpha and omega of Plato's "social creed," and it has the same ultimate effect as the Nomad or Eskimo *tour de force:* men end up by being slaves of habit, and progress is frozen.

One of man's persisting infirmities is to blame his failures on the operation of forces beyond his control. This maneuver, at first glance seemingly a gesture of humility, is in fact an indulgence in self-importance. The assumption that some major event in the universe is set in motion "in order to break one human career is among the most invidious of the Consolations of Philosophy. It is particularly attractive to sensitive minds in periods of decline and fall."[17]

Toynbee does not accept a loss of control over the physical environment as a valid reason for the decline of a civilization; likewise a loss of command over the human environment does not constitute a valid explanation. Toynbee's search for the cause or causes of the breakdown of a civilization leads to a series of negative findings. They are not acts of God. They are not the result of some "vain repetitions of senseless laws of Nature." They are not to be found in such matters as famines and floods, fires, and shipwrecks. By the "logical process of exhaustion," we are led to "return a verdict of suicide."

Two further mechanisms of stagnation require our attention: mimesis and idolatry. The trouble with mimesis is that it is not "self-determined." It is an action which a person or a culture would never have made "upon his own initiative." According to

Toynbee, "The weakness of mimesis lies in its being a mechanical response to a suggestion from an alien source."[18] It is more drill than inspiration. Toynbee would have a man, and a civilization, make it on its own.

Idolatry, as a technique of regression in a civilization, is given more weight in *A Study* than is mimesis. The nemesis of idolatry is more serious than the nemesis of mimesis, as these may be seen operating on the historical landscape. Religious idolatry is perhaps the most common and most serious of man's various idolatries:

> One of Man's fundamental and perennial errors—an error that is both an intellectual and a moral lapse—is to idolize discoveries of his own making that enhance his power. . . . The truth is that Anthropomorphism, even in its most ethereal expressions, is a form of idolatry if idolatry is to be defined as a worship of the creature instead of the Creator; and this worship of God in the image of Man—unlike the worship of God in an animal or in a stone—is also vitiated by the intellectual and moral failings of "the egocentric illusion". . . . Anthropomorphism seems likely to be harder for Man to transcend than any other form of idolatry because Man is the highest of God's creatures that is known to Man, and therefore, in so far as our knowledge of God Himself is derived from our knowledge of His creation, the image of God that is presented by Man is the least opaque fragment of the glass through which we see God darkly.[19]

Churches are especially susceptible to the danger of idolatry. A church lapses into this "worst form of all idolatry" when it believes that it is "not merely a depository of truth, but the sole depository of the whole truth in complete and definitive revelation of it."[20]

There are times when church and the state become enjoined into one grand idolatry. The reason behind Toynbee's great displeasure with Charlemagne's efforts at the restoration of the Holy Roman Empire is that this amounts to an idolatry of a past success rather than the fruits of one's own creative acts. Toynbee feels the same way about the Renaissance, which he views as a throwback to an earlier success. We cannot rest on our oars by admiring our own successes, nor can we hope to progress by an idolatry of an earlier success not of our own making. Both ways lead to regression and breakdown.

In our era, for better or worse, it is the intellectuals who assume the role of the internal minority. It is possible that this role may be taken over by a religious group and so effect something of a vindication of Toynbee's religious bias, as well as a vindication of his dynamics of history. We may see in the Berrigan brothers some suggestion of this possibility. However, in our day one would conclude that, when religious men achieve an eminence, they seem to be acting more like intellectuals than like the Christian internal proletariat of the Roman Empire. Tillich, Niebuhr, Maritain, Gilson, Dawson, and Buber may be classified with Lippmann, Russell, Sartre, and Camus more readily than with any late-twentieth-century equivalent of such men as Luther, Loyola, and Calvin.

A look at our immediate past suggests that the role of the creative minority was briefly monopolized by the Communists. Now, whatever may be the effectiveness of the New Left, one is safe in assuming in the West that Communists rarely serve the function of an internal proletariat. Or at best, we may say that the New Left or communism, whether Mao-inspired or Fanon-inspired or even Marx-inspired, is an uncertain force. The creative fire has gone and force has become its surrogate for creativeness. This is not to deny individual examples of creativeness.

Perhaps the pendulum is doomed to swing from the political extremity of the Communist Left to the nonpolitical extremity of religious prophecy. There are those who hold that the present period is one given over to superstition and irrationality. One example, perhaps, would be the Jesus freak, a kind of Christological hippie. Some run to religion because of the frightful use of science in this era. Lewis Mumford says, "The fruits of rationality can be misused for the pursuit of wicked and disastrous objectives. This is one of the reasons for the violent revulsions against rationality in our day, and it was one of the reasons for it in the last chapter of the history of the Greco-Roman world."[21] One may have to concede that today an intellectual may be found at both the polar extremes of rationality and irrationality.

Whether rational or irrational, what is the function of an intellectual? I suppose no one has tried harder to examine carefully the role of the intellectual than Karl Mannheim. He defines the "intelligentsia" as that group which tries to provide an interpretation of the world. Two things characterized the early intellectual. First, he belonged to a caste which enjoyed a monopoly position in molding a society's world view. Second, this caste operated in "relative remoteness from the open conflicts of everyday life."

Today there is no single caste or social stratum which supplies the members of this class. Further, no single class or caste has a monopolistic control of thought such as existed in the medieval church.

The disappearance of the caste and monopoly attributes has, according to Mannheim, made for a big change in the status of the intellectual. The intellectual today is drawn from many classes.

Intellectual work is no longer the sole responsibility of a "socially rigidly defined class, such as a priesthood, but rather by a social stratum which is to a large degree unattached to any social class." This condition creates the modern mind which turns its back on the finished authority of a priesthood and thinks rather in dynamic elastic terms.[22]

Since the intellectuals are drawn from many social classes, a certain restlessness has come to prevail. We have as a result what Mannheim refers to as the emergence of a "multiplicity of thought-styles." This restiveness is now seen as a "professional privilege."

We see a situation in which each intellectual brings with him his own social class biases and his own particular point of view. Mannheim has tried to identify five political orientations with which an intellectual might wish to affiliate: bureaucratic conservatism, conservative historicism, liberal-democratic thought, socialist-communist thought, and fascism.[23] We now have "an unanchored, relatively classless stratum" whose one unifying bond is "participation in a common educational heritage."

The emergence of these new classless intellectuals has made for some advantages. For one thing, they "transformed the conflict of interest into a conflict of ideas," according to Mannheim.[24] We increasingly resolved our disputes without resort to force or coercion. Since this class comes from many socioeconomic levels, and since it brings along a multiplicity of views, the prospect of "total perspective" becomes a possibility. We are able to look at problems from many angles. No single frame of reference is the lone sacred one.

Modern society finds itself engaged in a questioning process which "creates a uniquely modern propensity to reach behind and beyond appearances and to explode any fixed frame of reference which relies on ultimates." We have an intelligentsia which brings forward "as many points of view as are inherent in its varied social background." This is quite different from an earlier intelligentsia, the priesthood, says Mannheim: "The caste-secure scholastic built a stationary and compact edifice of concepts, in accordance with his stabilized existence. He raised only questions to which he already had answers. He expressed doubts in order to dispel them, and he did not sensitize himself to facts which would not confirm his convictions."[25] Even that methodical doubter, Descartes, knew when to stop his doubting.

If we may assume that neither a religious nor a political dominant minority will enforce a restriction on thought, then we may assume a continuing rich intellectual life. The educated, declares Mannheim, "no longer constitute a caste or a compact rank, but an open stratum. . . . No longer can any unitary view of the world become regnant, and the authoritarian habit of thinking in a closed scholastic system gives way to what we may call an intellectual process."[26] Mannheim's optimism may have been premature. Since his day we have heard from Herbert Marcuse about a one-dimensional man and from Jacques Ellul about a technology that flattens man out like a steam iron going over a pair of trousers.

In Mannheim, it is this coming together of many social strata which produces the intelligentsia. In Toynbee, it is something else; in him, it is the encounter between two civilizations which gives us the intelligentsia. There is a certain hazard in this thesis, namely, the prospect that soon the world might display but one civilization, the Western one. But that amalgamation has not yet occurred. In truth, Toynbee finds the present quite favorable for creating minorities to serve an intellectual function not unlike that which we find in Mannheim.

Our present situation overwhelms us with its potentiality for creating minorities as the West continues to engulf ten disintegrating civilizations. While engaging in this recruitment of personnel from civilizations in a state of decline, the West has "swallowed up almost all the primitive societies." Toynbee holds that we are confronted on this score with an *embarras de richesses*.[27]

Toynbee pushes his functional description of the intelligentsia somewhat further than Mannheim. Today millions of persons have been "uprooted and disoriented spiritually" while continuing to live in their ancestral homes. In this situation, there is need for a special class "to serve as a human counterpart to the 'transformer' which changes an electric current from one voltage to another." Toynbee would call these transformers, these liaison officers between cultures, the intelligentsia.[28]

The first persons to learn "the trick of an intrusive civilization's trade" are the army and navy officers. Peter the Great of Russia was, in this sense, a member of this class. He had to learn the military technologies of the West to save Russia from being conquered by the military forces of Sweden. The next to play this role is the diplomatic corps; then, the merchants; and finally those whom Toynbee considers to be the most characteristic types: the schoolmaster, the civil servant, and the lawyer. The schoolmaster teaches Western subject matter to his fellow countrymen. The civil servant learns the administrative pattern of the West and the lawyer its legal process.

The presence of an intelligentsia is evidence that two civilizations have been in contact and that one is absorbing the other. The member of the intelligentsia is the one who belongs wholly to neither of these two civilizations: "This liaison-class suffers from the congenital unhappiness of the bastard and the hybrid, who is an outcast from both families—or a sport in both races —that have guiltily combined to beget him. An intelligentsia is hated and despised by its own people because its very existence is a reproach to them."[29] Today, in the West and perhaps elsewhere, we have alienated youth by reaping this hatred.

An intelligentsia is born to be unhappy. A member of it fits Toynbee's definition of the proletariat. He is in but not of the two societies. He is not Mannheim's intellectual, but he has this much in common with him: he is not a member of a hereditary caste. He is the outcast, the outsider, the ill-at-ease, the marginal. The success of Mannheim's intellectual results from his capacity to view things from the vantage point of total perspective. Toynbee's succeeds by virtue of mimesis: "the essence of the intelligentsia's profession is, after all, mimesis," which becomes his *tour de force*. "The border-line of contact and fusion between one disintegrating civilization and another" is congenial soil for mimesis. While doomed to unhappiness, while liked by neither culture, the prospect of serving as a liaison-officer is attractive. Its disadvantages are offset by "its prestige in the eyes of those who are eligible for enrollment in it." As a matter of fact, this condition makes it so attractive that in no time at all we have an oversupply of candidates for this class. As their numbers increase, so does their unhappiness.

This internal minority is a threat to the dominant minority which lacks the creative ability to educate in its own right. Toynbee relates how upon his arrival in Japan in 1929 he had to reveal all the books he had with him. He felt the reason for this precaution was the uncertainty of the ruling class in Japan.[30]

Contact between two cultures is the major mechanism for creating an intelligentsia, but it is not the only such process. It may occur within a single culture. We can see a "Western internal proletariat being recruited from the native tissues of the Western body social."[31] This happens, as it did in Germany, when too many persons are educated without supplying them with an outlet for their skills. This could be the situation in the United States in the 1970's. It is then that the intellectuals look for the man on the white horse. In Germany, the educated unemployed got Hitler.

In the West, especially in the United States, we may see the intellectual being absorbed into the commodity and advertising segments of a consumer society. C. Wright Mills finds the intellectual in default: he escapes major issues by flight into abstract theories or by an internment in the statistical ritual. Herbert Marcuse and Michael Harrington see him as seduced by a system which delivers the goods on a grand scale: in short, all the comforts of suburbia. As someone has put it, from 1945 to 1970 the carrots were real.

Toynbee sees rebellion emerging from technological advancement. Technological organization and rationalization will bring about a regime so repressive that men will be driven to take desperate steps.

While technology has liberated man's economic activities from the cycles of day and night and of the seasons, it has enslaved mankind on another plane. Our ancient servitude to the stars has been replaced by a new servitude to man. Once nonhuman nature acted as a buffer between man and man. Now that buffer has been removed, and man is brought face to face with himself without that old challenge, namely nature.[32]

Even the moon has gone, and Norman Mailer can observe that "the psychology of machines begins where humans are more machinelike in their actions than the machines they employ."[33]

If one accepts Toynbee's thesis regarding the importance of an internal proletariat, then we have good reason for concern. The challenge from the physical environment has changed radically since the time when it served as the factor which effected the transition of a primitive society into a primary civilization.

Perhaps an event like the discovery of atomic energy creates an internal minority. In a sense, the atomic scientists since Hiroshima constitute an internal minority. The atomic scientist in his disenchantment and fear over the bomb is an outsider. NASA (National Aeronautics and Space Administration) officials and the astronauts could be another. They would be neither wholly of this world nor of space. Robert Jay Lifton suggests that the survivors of the atomic-bomb attack in Japan could very well prove to be a kind of internal minority. Yet one must ask: would any of these groups compare with the status of the early Christians in the Roman Empire?

We find ourselves living in a Westernized world. There are no barbarians who threaten us from beyond some frontier. The Russian and Chinese Communists seem as committed to Western materialism as any cartel of international bankers. India seems to be moving in the same direction. Encounters between civilizations which would produce an intelligentsia are becoming increasingly improbable. "The virtual elimination of external challenges from the human environment . . . has been one of the remarkable features of our Western history," says Toynbee.[34] Paul Valery adds: "The age of free expansion is at an end. There is not a rock without its flag, there are no more blanks on the map, no region beyond law and custom. . . . The age of a finite world is now beginning."[35] For Michael Harrington "what is incontestable and momentous is that the West, for the first time in its history, is not fundamentally challenged from within."[36] This is a different West. Perhaps now we must seek our encounters between generations; the generation gap becomes our new mechanism, the counterculture of youth our hope.

In a Westernized technicalized ecumenical world, what must one do to be saved? Where are we to turn for the transfiguring power? How does one withdraw in a world where every rock has its flag, where every beach and every mountain is a resort area? Perhaps we are already beyond salvation. Toynbee frequently hints that we may be at the universal stage in our development, a stage that according to the history Toynbee both reads and writes, can only advance to stagnation and disintegration. Toynbee's worries on this point are based on the status of internal minorities in our society.

The civil-servant class, once an important segment in our intelligentsia, is now playing it safe. Its members display "a lack of zest, a disinclination to take the initiative or to incur risks, and an impulse to play for personal safety."[37] The middle class is going too: ". . .in the twentieth century, the temperature of this Western middle-class psychic energy [has been] reduced to a milder degree through the conversion of the children of predatory buccaneers and entrepreneurs into conscientious civil servants and employees of giant non-governmental business concerns."[38] As for the working classes, in their fight to resist the regimentation of the owners and the machines they have only succeeded in regimenting themselves anew into unions. Once robots in the factory system, they have become robots in the trade-union movement. And beyond this lay another robot trap, says Toynbee: "Mankind might then have to reckon with the possibility that a Mechanized Technology might contain within itself the psychic seeds of its own decay."[39]

Some have looked to education to save us—not so Toynbee. We have seen "the inevitable impoverishment in the intellectual results of Education when the process is reduced to its elements and is divorced from its traditional social and cultural background in order to make it available for 'the masses.' "[40] Our democratic aspirations in education have not been able to bring off the miracle of the loaves and fishes. Toynbee seems to accept the social law "that learning is sterilized by diffusion." Withal he is able to resurrect a touch of optimism regarding education: "If these attempts to adjust the system of Education to the impact of Democracy achieve some degree of success within some measurable time, then our Western Society may still succeed in steering its hazardous educational course through the narrow fairway between a Northcliffian Scylla and a Hitlerian Charybdis; but at the present moment the fortunes of our perilous voyage are still in doubt."[41]

Technology holds forth even less hope than education. Toynbee asks whether mankind, when it succumbed to the enchantment of technology, sentenced itself to live in a "Brave New World" the rest of its days. He suggests that the guests at Circe's banquet may find themselves penned in her sty. Yet Toynbee finds hope in what he calls "this angelically or demonically spiritual strain" in human nature. This spiritual dimension may keep men from becoming the complete prisoners of technology's sty.[42] Again, Toynbee's answer leaves us with a modicum of hope; there is that small chance.

In more than one sense, *A Study* ends with volume nine; the last paragraph in that volume reads:

Gibbon's unargued assumption that progress in Technology and progress in morals must run neck and neck, as a matter of course, had been so effectively refuted by the experience of 170 more years of Western history that it could not fail to be evident to a Western historian, taking an observation in A.D. 1952, that progress in Technology, so far from being a guarantee of progress in virtue and happiness, was a challenge to it. Each time that Man increased the potency of his material tools, he was increasing the gravity of the moral consequences of his acts and thereby raising the minimum standard of goodness required of him if his growing power was not to turn to his destruction; and, while it was true that, in so far as a human soul succeeded in meeting Technology's spiritual challenge, technological progress might be credited with having been at least the blind and unintentional stimulus of this spiritual achievement, it was also true, as we have observed, that each individual soul had to fight the same ever recurring spiritual battle for itself under a mounting pressure from a Technology whose collective and therefore cumulative progress was bearing ever harder on each individual human spirit. In the intolerably mechanized "Brave New World" conjured into existence by the Western Civilization in its post-Modern Age it was hard indeed for any human soul to resist the temptation of becoming a fiend without succumbing to the opposite temptation of becoming a robot. This was the Human Race's predicament as twentieth-century Western eyes saw it, and from this observation no facilely pleasing conclusion could be drawn.[43]

Having told his story in this manner, is it any wonder that Toynbee would turn to religion? Where else could he turn if this is his conclusion: "The meaning behind the facts of History which the poetry in the facts is leading us is a revelation of God and a hope of communion with Him"?[44]

Thus Toynbee had written in 1954. In 1966 he wrote: "In this coming age of mechanization, atomic power, affluence, and leisure, religion will surely come into its own as the one boundless field for freedom and for creativity that is open for the unlimited aspirations of human nature."[45] This, he says, would be a hard saying for modern Western man, and it might prove to be even harder for the non-Western intelligentsia who are trying so diligently to emulate Western man. Man has been concentrating on mastering nonhuman nature. He had allowed his "gift for spiritual contemplation to grow rusty through disuse. It will be painful and terrifying for him to reverse the modern tide of Western life and to look inward again."[46] In 1970, Toynbee declared that men "have made the tragic mistake of seeking an antidote to the failure of rationality by cultivating irrationality for its own sake. . . . What they ought to have done was not to have jettisoned rationality but to have dedicated themselves to love."[47]

In 1954, it is God; in 1966, it is turning inward; in 1970, it is love, with rationality unjettisoned. It seems to me that it would be scarcely fair to comment on the seeming inconsistencies of these varied exhortations coming from the pen of a self-proclaimed agnostic. Toynbee is easy to disagree with; probably no one has been disagreed with so much as our historian. Hence, rather than engage in yet another disagreement with the author of *A Study of History*, it would seem much more appropriate at this stage to examine Toynbee's process of change—the creative minority—as an antidote for the crushing impact of technologism and consumerism in our day.

The theme of a triumphant technology becoming man's master is a common one in the nuclear age. If we turn to Herbert Marcuse, we read:

The very idea of a non-repressive civilization, conceived as a real possibility of the established civilization at the present stage, appears frivolous. Even if one admits this possibility on theoretical grounds, an extension of the achievements of science and technology, one must be aware of the fact that these same achievements are being used to the contrary, namely, to serve the interests of continued domination. The modes of domination have changed: they have become increasingly technological, productive, and even beneficial; consequently, in the most advanced areas of industrial society, the people have been co-ordinated and reconciled with the system of domination to an unprecedented degree.[48]

This system which "delivers the goods" seems capable of "containing social change." This system "tends to become totalitarian to the extent to which it determines not only the socially needed occupations, skills, and attitudes, but also individual needs and aspirations."[49] We cannot distinguish between private and public needs. We carry on in "voluntary servitude."

Michael Harrington in *The Accidental Century* goes over much the same ground. We are living in a revolutionary period, only we do not have any revolutionaries about to guide us. The poor have no voice; they have been bribed by the commodities of the industrial order. As we have noted above, Harrington holds that for the first time in its history the West is not challenged from within. Harrington refers to Toynbee on this very point. According to Toynbee, the poor should have withdrawn from society. But they did not. Harrington then asks: "What happens if there is an integration of the proletariat rather than a secession?"[50] The question is rhetorical.

Whatever may be the condition of the world, it seems to me there is reason for moderate hope (the moderation theme in Albert Camus perhaps) in Toynbee's mechanisms of withdrawal and return, that is, in the creative impact of internal minorities. Marcuse feels that blacks or students may prove to be this very minority; but the student movement cannot be considered a truly revolutionary force so long as there are no masses capable or willing to follow. It may, however, serve as a hope that there is an alternative. The student movement testifies to "the real possibility of a free society."[51] The student rebellion of the 1960's rejected both Western capitalism and Eastern communism. As we approach the mid-1970's, one may well wonder if this youth movement is not already a thing of the past. Consciousness III is now nostalgia.

Toynbee indulges in some moderately optimistic remarks in *Reconsiderations,* when he writes that "human freedom is not non-determination; it is self-determination."[52] Freedom remains genuine within its apparent limits. We get some hints of what freedom means when we view an encounter between man and his environment as a heuristic intellectual activity. What Toynbee is suggesting here is that an encounter between civilizations is not the sole inspiration for intellectual activity and that an encounter between man and his environment may also serve this function. If this is true, then we may assume that some intellectual activity, some potential for freedom, will remain with us even if we should merge our planet into a single Westernized civilization.

We may use Toynbee's phraseology to describe and analyze our contemporary era. It is reasonable to suppose that our technology is our *tour de force.* We are frozen in no less than the Eskimo with his kayak or the nomad with his horse. We are one-dimensional. It is possible to think of the youthful members of our counterculture as a creative minority hard at work challenging our dominant minority, the establishment. We have substituted "the adolescentization of dissent" for "the proletarianization of dissent," according to Theodore Roszak: "For the young have become one of the very few social levers dissent has to work with. This is that significant soil in which the Great Refusal has begun to take root."[53] Roszak refers to this refusal on the part of the young as an invasion of the centaurs. (His metaphor is not a wholly happy one in the context of Toynbee's various *tours de force.*) The counterculture thus precipitated on the scene is defined as "a culture so radically disaffiliated from the mainstream assumptions of our society that it scarcely looks to many as a culture at all, but takes on the alarming appearance of a barbaric intrusion."[54]

Surely many must see Woodstock as a barbaric intrusion. Equally surely many must view the long-haired unkempt youth in the protest lines as barbarians. But they are not barbarians (the external proletariat); rather they are the creative minority with some religious overtones (the internal proletariat). They are uniquely the products of technology, space travel, nuclear warfare, and electronic communications. They are uniquely the sons and daughters of the power elite, who developed and who run the establishment. They are internal. They are creative.

Leonard Woolf has this to say: "The perpetual tragedy of history is that things are perpetually being done ten or twenty years too late."[55] Perhaps our centaurs have come on the scene too late. Perhaps only an external proletariat now striving for a tribal ecological balance in remote Africa and Asia can bring off the new effort. And that triumph would not be the triumph of Western technology and Western democracy but something quite different.

CHAPTER 5

Reconsiderations *Considered*

H ISTORIANS, who are given to recording the great deeds of kings, nations, and civilizations, have not been averse to recording the minutiae of their own lives. Perhaps the historical and the autobiographical are but two slightly diverse tendencies of a single more inclusive disposition. Two autobiographies stand out: Edward Gibbon's and Henry Adams's. In each, one may say that the autobiographical effort enjoys an eminence quite as distinguished as the historical effort.

Gibbon begins his autobiography on a joyful note: "In the fifty-second year of my age, after the completion of an arduous and successful work, I now propose to employ some moments of my leisure in reviewing the simple transactions of a private and literary life. . . . My own amusement is my motive, and will be my reward."[1] Henry Adams begins the story of his life with a hint of failure: "Probably no child, born in the year (1838), held better cards than he. . . . As it happened, he never got to the point of playing the game at all; he lost himself in the study of it, watching the errors of the players."[2]

Toynbee, too, has given us autobiography: *Acquaintances* (1967) and *Experiences* (1969). As Gibbon so delightedly puts it, we like to "enlarge the narrow circle in which nature has confined us" and we do this by filling up "the silent vacancy that precedes our birth, by associating ourselves to the authors of our existence."[3] And this is precisely what Toynbee does in *Acquaintances*. It is a look at Uncle Harry, Auntie Charlie (Charlotte), Sir Alfred Zimmern, the Webbs, Jan Smuts, T. E. Lawrence, and others. In *Experiences*, Toynbee becomes "the subject as well as the narrator."

In engaging in autobiography, Toynbee, then, follows a pattern not uncommon among historians. In *Reconsiderations* (1961), he seems to break new ground; or, in any event, there is a massive quality to *Reconsiderations* which makes it unique among the autobiographical writings of historians and, one may suppose, among all autobiographies. As one reads this book, one soon gets the impression that Toynbee has determinedly replied to every critic who ever laid a verbal hand on *A Study of History*. Indeed, he seems to respond to every single criticism of every critic, favorable or unfavorable. This is, of course, not wholly true; but surely this is the impression this book leaves with the reader.

Other authors seem content to write new prefaces for successive editions and to take some cognizance of what critics have had to say about a particular book in these prefaces. Not so Toynbee. *Reconsiderations* runs to over 700 pages. In response to the opinion of others, he explains or revises the usage of twenty-eight key terms ranging from metahistory to agnosticism. The geneses of the Egyptian, Indic, Chinese, Andean, and pre-Columbian civilizations are restated. There are headings such as "The Heuristic Use of Hypotheses," "The Issue between Trans-Rationalists and Rationalists," and "Attempts to Bridge the Gap between our Knowledge of Psychic and Social Phenomena and our Knowledge of the Acts of Individual Human Beings." The bibliography of critical commentaries runs to over 200 entries.

The voluminousness of *Reconsiderations* is commensurate with the voluminousness of *A Study of History*. What is more, Toynbee means this book of responses to be an integral part of *A Study*; it constitutes volume XII of *A Study*.

When volumes VII, VIII, IX, and X appeared, Peter Geyl confessed that at the sight of those 2,500 pages his heart sank. "But it was inevitable that I should find my way through that strange and yet familiar country."[4]

Thus when *Reconsiderations* came off the press, my heart sank. I had suffered through Toynbee's big switch in volume VII when he substituted higher religion for civilization as his intelligible unit of history. Somehow one had comforted himself that, with volume X, *A Study of History* had at last come to an end, and that henceforth the Toynbee devotee could relax with the expectation of having to worry about little more than casual books from the pen of Arnold Toynbee.

But now one had to face up to the fact that Toynbee had written a long book of reconsiderations in which he had weakened his stand on some issues, added a slight nuance to the meaning of this or that word, wondered whether he had ignored some obscure historian's contribution to the authoritative body of knowledge on the rise of the Syriac civilization, complained that his classical education may have been the reason for prejudicial views concerning the West, etc. With all these changes would one now have to go back and read A *Study of History* from start to finish? To anyone with a modicum of family, instructional, or societal responsibility, there would be only one reply: Oh, no!

It would be presumptuous for one to advise another to read A *Study*. To do this is the equivalent of asking a scholar who reads a great deal to surrender something on the order of six to eight months of his reading time; for a less diligent scholar, we are talking about giving up something in excess of a year. Under any circumstances, we are dealing with a major assignment.

But we may ask a lesser question: if one has read the ten volumes of A *Study*, should one read *Reconsiderations*? Yes, by all means. Why? A *Study* is the progressive revelation of a personality. It would be a mistake to conclude that revelation prematurely by a failure to read *Reconsiderations*. The same holds true for *Acquaintances* and *Experiences*.

Martin Duberman has observed that "historians tend not to be interested in personality. . . . [They are] more concerned with how man functions and performs in society than how man lives alone with himself."[5] While I should be reluctant to present Toynbee as the historian who directly contradicts this statement by Duberman, I would hold that, although Toynbee may not make personality central in A *Study*, the personality of Toynbee himself is central to A *Study* and to *Reconsiderations*.

I

It is safe to assert that no book has ever been subject to so much harsh and unfavorable criticism as A *Study of History*. Some of this takes place on the rarified heights of historical esoterica; a good deal of it is theological; some of it is stylistic. The range is wide and deep. Whether our concern is to measure the amount or the variety, there is but one conclusion; no one has been so variously and so massively criticized as Arnold J. Toynbee. Great minds have praised him, and great minds have made fun of him. And the same can be said of the little minds.

To some, Toynbee emerges as an intellectual giant, as a profound prophetic voice. To others, he is a silly nincompoop.

Toynbee has stature; he is a major figure in the twentieth century. Yet, when we weight the criticisms of him, we seem forced to conclude that by far the larger part has been unkind, unfavorable, and destructive. We have this sort of thing: "Dr. Toynbee is a fine product of the traditional English education which studied only dead civilizations and disliked contact with life."[6] He is an "expatriate, a rootless man; alien everywhere as a result, at home only among ruins. He sees history as an endless round of conquest and superstition. He never sees people."[7] Marguerite Howe finds *A Study* a "speculative philosophy of history, whose immense scope is only slightly less staggering than its author's naivete." To her, it is a "myoptic overview."[8] Another level of criticism is represented by the following: "But the closer Toynbee comes to the facts, the less convincing he is about the reality of civilizations."[9] The *Manchester Guardian* editorial staff in a tribute to Toynbee on his seventieth birthday suggested the range of commentary: "The philosopher-historian who has been variously hailed as one of the most remarkable minds of our age and, at the other extreme, dismissed as the author of 3,000,000 words of unreadable fantasy."[10]

Toynbee knew it would come. *Reconsiderations* begins:

In publishing a book a writer is deliberately exposing his work to "the wreckful siege of battering days". This is his own doing. He has been under no compulsion, except an inner one. But, having once published, he must then choose between two alternative policies. He can say, 'What I have written, I have written', and spend the rest of his working life on trying to maintain his previous positions—for no better reason than that he happens once to have occupied them. Alternatively, he can think again; see whether or not he has changed his mind on this or that disputed point. . . .[11]

Here it is a siege. Elsewhere he calls criticism "pummellings": "Their pummellings have given me a mental massage that has loosened the joints and muscles of my mind and has set it moving on a new course."[12] He compares encountering his critics to "venturing into a mine-field." He sees critics as hawks who "will swoop down on his published work like kites, and with kites' eyes

for the weak points in it."[13] Reading critics has had the "depress-
ing effect of taking daily doses of weed-killer."

Toynbee says some critics write with such animosity that their
first concern "is to draw blood." But one can learn from one's critics, and Toynbee takes great pains to thank them: "I am also in-
debted to my critics. But for them, this volume would not have
been written." Toynbee is not lacking in fluency when discussing
criticism:

I have profited particularly from reviews that have been severe without
being hostile. The value of a review also depends on the reviewer's way
of working. Some critics work with the road-metalworker's hammer.
Sometimes it is the stone that breaks, sometimes, perhaps, the
hammer-head. In either case the result is on the small scale, and its
value, while appreciable, is limited. A more creative kind of criticism is
the kind that blows in like a sand-laden wind from the desert; for this
usefully transforms the landscape. It finds out the softer rocks and scours
them away, and it grinds down the harder rocks' sharp edges. Anything
that still stands after this wind has done its testing work will be that
much closer to reality.[14]

O. H. K. Spate gives Toynbee a hard time on some geographical
conclusions in A Study. In reply Toynbee proves himself the
English gentleman he is sometimes accused of being: "However, my
concern with Spate is, not to return his fire, but to follow out the
second thoughts into which I have been stung by the stimulating
shot with which he has peppered me."[15] We discover Toynbee
treating a critic, D. M. Robinson, now dead, in this gentle tone:
"In self-defense, I have to point these inaccuracies [in Robinson]
out, though I feel rueful about having to do this when Robinson
is no longer in this world to stand up for himself."[16]

Toynbee takes all of this quite in his stride—quite philosophi-
cally as we say. He holds that it is "more profitable to try to learn
from one's critics than to try to fight them." He is glad that his
critics have kept him alive at sea instead of stagnating in port.
They have prevented him from committing "intellectual suicide":

I mean to go on pursuing my search, but I do not expect it to bring me
to an "end", and if I found myself "in port" I should be distressed. Man's
quest is really an attempt to probe to the heart of the mystery of the
Universe, and I do not believe that human beings can attain that goal in

this life. If a port on this side of death is unattainable, it is best to keep to the seas. One does this, of course, at one's peril.[17]

We can understand that by "pursuing my search" Toynbee means to continue to study history and to continue to study what his critics have had to say.

Toynbee has not been out to draw blood from his critics, and considering how his critics have been at him, this is an achievement of considerable merit.

II

More than one intellectual has been dismissed from the scholars' club with the phrase "just for a handful of silver he left us." The phrase is not quite appropriate for Toynbee, and historians have been hard put to find a clear case for reading Toynbee out of the ranks of the historian. Rather unfortunately in this context, he has been for some decades the most eminent historian. He is one of the few with world-wide renown. He stands rather alone and above the others. "It can be safely asserted that Toynbee has had a greater influence on informed opinion than any historian of his generation,"[18] declares one critic.

Here is the *representative* historian in the eyes of the public, to use Emerson's expression, and yet the historians just do not care for him. He has gone too far. Just for a bucketful of theology he left us. Just for a tubful of philosophy he left us.

Historians, in general, hold that historians should not engage in philosophy, and "it is partly because Arnold Toynbee has insisted on transcending this self-imposed limitation on his craft that he has become so controversial a figure among his peers."[19]

He not only transcends "the proper function," he just is not careful enough. He displays such unprofessional conduct as "intuitive leaps," and a "disdain for system," and he goes in for such unpardonable things as "literary looseness of phrase" and "evocative and persuasive style." Further, this whole enterprise is "undermined by the unclarity of his conception of what he is trying to verify."[20]

This steady stream of unfavorable comment by fellow-historians disturbs Toynbee. Masur writes of *Reconsiderations:* "Toynbee, at length, takes heed of these criticisms; he reviews them in this

volume with open and impartial mind, and with a candor which
reveals, if nothing else, an extraordinary degree of intellectual
honesty."[21] We see this candor early in volume XII:

These excesses of mine—if I am guilty of excesses—evidently deserve
the notice, and the reproof, that they have received. But my plan of
work has not only drawn reasoned criticisms of the way in which I have
carried it out; it has also provoked strong, and even violent, hostility
among a considerable number of my fellow historians. It has been noted
that in the United States I was ill received by extremely distinguished
reviewers—e.g. Charles A. Beard and Lynn Thorndike—in the important professional journals. This reaction has not been peculiar to American scholars; I am conscious of an even stronger current of hostile feeling
among British and Dutch scholars, and also of a more aloof distaste and
disapproval among French scholars. This vein of emotion has surprised
and puzzled me. At first sight it seems uncalled-for in an intellectual argument; for in this field emotion is not only irrelevant but notoriously
inimical to clear thinking. . . . If the distinguished scholars who have
hurled thunderbolts at me had merely felt annoyed with me personally,
they would just have ignored me, which would have been a more effective way of trying to dispose of me than the policy of anathematizing me
which they have actually adopted. I believe that the strength of their
feeling reveals that they felt themselves to be fighting about something
much more important than anything merely personal. They are, I think,
up in arms in defense of the uniqueness of historical events and human
personalities. This is, in their eyes, a treasure of supreme value; and my
work has been a red flag to them because they have taken it as a symbol
of an attack on the principle of respect for the element of uniqueness in
history which they value so highly.[22]

This underplaying of uniqueness and an acceptance of some
element of uniformity is one red flag; but perhaps there is an
even redder flag, namely, Toynbee's insistence that his method of
studying history is "empirical" or "scientific." "In the two and a
half decades since Toynbee's *Study* began to appear it has received criticism of a number of kinds," according to William
Dray. "The hard core of that criticism, however, has generally
been in one way or another the claim of 'scientific' status for his
conclusions is bogus, and perhaps irretrievably so."[23] In an almost too typically Toynbeean manner Toynbee introduces his reconsideration of "empirical" with an erudite listing of the Greek
origins of this word. While claiming that his method is empirical,
he is not claiming that his approach is "without preconceptions."

There is simply no way of avoiding some theoretical framework, for "the human mind's process of thought is analytical and classificatory."[24]

Toynbee has been accused of carelessness in his use of historical facts, but withal he is history's most generous footnoter and indexer. In one footnote he makes reference to sixteen persons who have questioned his use of the term "empirical" to describe his method. Toynbee may not come to grips with his critics at all times, but he does give them recognition. Further, he does explain what he means by "empirical":

When Trevor-Roper says that, in my work, "the theories are not deduced from the facts", the answer is that neither my theories nor anyone else's are or ever have been or ever will be generated in that way. If being "empirical" meant this, the word would have no counterpart in reality, and had better be struck out of the dictionary. . . . I agree that my claim cannot be sustained if I have not tried to test my theories and hypotheses by the facts, or if I have tried but have not done the job properly or successfully. For, while it is true that theories and hypotheses can never be deduced from facts, it is also true that they can be validated only if they are confronted with relevant facts and are confirmed by them. More than that, the whole purpose of formulating a theory or an hypothesis is the heuristic one of trying to increase our knowledge and understanding by applying the theory or hypothesis to the phenomena. I maintain my claim that I have tried to be empirical in this sense, which is, I believe, the only correct usage of the word and does mean something that an inquirer not only can be but ought to be.[25]

The battle will rage on: is Toynbee's method empirical or not? I do not care to reenter the fray at this stage. And what is more, Toynbee suggests that the answer may lie in the subconscious, and to this Toynbee has a definitive reply: "I do not know how to clear myself of a charge against my subconscious."[26]

Isaiah Berlin has written about the difficulties of being a historian. Unlike the natural scientists, the historians have to reconstruct the past in terms of their own theories and categories, but they must also attend to how historical events were seen by those who participated in them. They have to be aware of "psychological facts that in their turn themselves influences events."[27]

Present-day physicists and chemists "are not obliged to investigate the states of mind of Lavoisier or Boyle." Tonybee suggests that we will have to pry into the subconscious of historians. A rather impossible task in the case of Herodotus and Gibbon. However, we could get underway with living historians if only psychiatrists were not already so overworked with sick patients. When things let up a little, we may hear the battle cry: historians, prepare to meet your psychiatrist.

Another area of common criticism of Toynbee by historians is his comprehensive, universal, ecumenical, generalized approach—his panoramic view of history. Toynbee reconsiders this charge. His defense is sincere and by and large effective:

My quarrel is not with the civil servants; it is with scholars who gratuitously import the bureaucratic state of mind into the field of intellectual inquiry.

In this field the bureaucratic approach is not only incongruous; it is obstructive; for, in intellectual inquiry, freedom is the breath of life and formalism is, not a safeguard, but a shackle. There is nothing to be said for breaking up the study of human affairs into the so-called "disciplines." These have grown up haphazard, independently of each other. In consequence there are overlaps between them and also gaps that are covered by none of them. The relations between them have never been reviewed or revised on a rational plan. Indeed, any suggestion that this should be done would be likely to arouse hot opposition. The feeling between the votaries of the different intellectual disciplines is almost as bad as it is between the adherents of the different higher religions. There are historians, for instance, who do not admit that sociology is a legitimate form of study, or who, if they do admit this, do so only on the proviso that the two disciplines are to be deemed to have nothing to do with each other—a fantastic notion, considering that history and sociology are concerned with the study of the same affairs. There are philosophers, again, who take up a corresponding attitude toward psychology.

Such attitudes are not only absurd but obscurantist. . . . When each discipline draws in its horns and tries to turn itself into a Leibnizian "monad", intellectual progress is being sabotaged; for there can be no exchange of ideas between the inmates of windowless houses; and the cutting of interdisciplinary communications is the more damaging because the traditional boundary walls between the disciplines are unplanned and arbitrary. . . . These conventional barriers are particularly cramping at a time, such as that through which we are now living, in which knowledge and understanding are in flux, and in which successive increases in both of them are making repeated revolutionary changes in the configuration of the whole of our intellectual landscape.[28]

This attitude is absurd and obscurantist and Toynbee sends out a call for a "ruthless demolition squad, armed with the intellectual equivalent of atomic artillery, to batter the traditional interdisciplinary walls to the ground."[29] He wants the partitions to be provisional at best. Each of us must attempt "to take a panoramic view of the whole field." It is only in this way that we can come "as near as possible to seeing Reality as it is." This must be our approach if we would arrive at any understanding of human affairs.

Toynbee himself would have us look at reality in a binocular way: the large panoramic view and the small myopic one. Masur feels that *A Study of History* has captured the public imagination because of Toynbee's conviction "that history stands in need of the two complementary approaches, the microscopic and the macroscopic." Toynbee stands his ground on both of these approaches and throws his answer into the faces of his critics.

He would look at reality as a whole and not in piecemeal fashion. There are those who criticize Toynbee for failing to make an exhaustive citation of examples. This criticism, he avers, hits him "less hard than some of my fellow prisoners in the dock, if it is true that I have surfeited my readers with examples *ad nauseam.*" Later in *Reconsiderations,* Toynbee rebukes scholars who "put all their faith and all their works too into specialization." Specialization has become an indispensable intellectual tool, but "being indispensable is not the same as being all-sufficient." A serious danger in specialization is that this approach leaves "unexplored gaps between the specialist's deep but narrowly constructed borings."[30] The scholar's work will be incomplete "if the microscopic approach is not supplemented by a panoramic one."[31]

In some respects Toynbee is the Rogerian among the historians—the permissive, undogmatic, open-self sort. He remains always the metaphorist. He views his job as an historian as that of a man "moving old furniture about." He adds, "For too long these pieces have been cluttering up attics." Toynbee assigns himself the "back-breaking job" of dragging these pieces out and arranging them in the hall. In this sense, Toynbee in his effort at a comprehensive history is doing the work of a pioneer, which is "to open up the jungle by blazing trails." Some may not like the trails that Toynbee has blazed, but let them at least credit him with heroic work. Some historians who quite disapprove of Toynbee do not have the courage to enter the historical jungles that Toynbee tackles in *A Study of History.*

Toynbee's plea is for a comprehensive history undertaken with a multidisciplined attack. This would be his answer to those who accuse him of being now a poet, now a prophet, now a philosopher:

> In the study of human affairs one cannot afford to neglect any approach. One must be free to resort to the different methods of the poet, the historian, and the scientist in turn, according to each piece of the task; and, in order to enjoy this freedom to use all the methods, it is best not to be tied to any of the corresponding names.[32]

"There is no such thing as a master-key that will unlock *all* doors." Hence we join forces. In our day we see "the merger of the old departmental 'disciplines' in a new comprehensive study of human affairs." Scientists perhaps see this as their problem too, and so we read an appeal from them: "Today, to meet the new needs of the entire species . . . the concepts and methods of all the sciences must be combined."[33] To save ourselves we have come together as people and as scholars. Toynbee asks that we subordinate our "traditional parochial loyalties to a new paramount loyalty to mankind itself." If this request is what Toynbee brings out of the jungle of unassembled historical pieces, if this comes from his blazing a path in the historical jungles, then would that others followed him instead of their narrow and nationalistic histories.

III

Toynbee tells his readers that in seeking to test the hypotheses presented in the 10 volumes of *A Study,* he made his net for collecting evidence "as big, and its meshes as close, as I have been able."[34] By and large his net has been a Hellenic one, and if the meshes were close, then we have to thank Toynbee for his wide and deep grasp of Greek civilization. Toynbee is quite frank in volume XII about his Hellenic bias. It resulted from the classical education he received. According to him, "A classical education may be defined as one in which the staple discipline is an initiation into some culture that is older than the present-day culture of the society in which this form of higher education is the established one."[35] Toynbee holds that this sort of education was not at all peculiar to the England in which he grew up. Indeed, it was the common education for most of the world over a period of some 400 or 500 years. It was standard procedure in China, India, Persia, Turkey, and the Arabic lands. "If 'classical' education has been one of Mankind's follies, it has, at any rate, not been a rare one," he states. And he explains if he had been born a Chinese lad instead of an English one, "I should have come in for a classical education that would have been almost identical down to such details as being taught to write essays in the 'classical' language and 'classical' style." This system of education persisted for years over a good part of the globe. Societies engaged in their second or third attempt at civilization "had arrived independently at this queer system of education." For all of its worldwide distribution and for all of its long-lasting qualities, it seems to have come to a close in England with Toynbee's generation: "My generation was almost the last in England to be given an education in the Greek and Latin languages and literature that remained faithful to the strictest fifteenth-century Italian standards."[36] According to Alfred North Whitehead, this was the generation that considered the Bible a Greek book.

Toynbee does not regret his classical education: "I find myself now, as ever, counting it as a piece of supreme good fortune that, being born, as I was, in England, I happened to be born there just early enough to come in for this education in an uncompromisingly complete version of it." The sovereign virtue in this type of education is that "the subject of it is human affairs."[37] But there are dangers present. While a good tool, it may be pushed too far and thus lead to distortions in the historian's perspective:

If a Western historian does not fall into the egocentric error of making all history lead up to the point reached in the West in his own generation, he is likely to fall into another error, only one degree less egocentric, with which I, for instance, have been charged, with some justice, by a number of my critics. He is likely to use Hellenic history, which lies in the background of his own Western history, as an exclusive "model", not just one out of a number of alternative possible models, for elucidating the configuration of history in general in the current age of the civilizations. Since the World is now being unified as a result of Western invention, and therefore, initially, within a Western framework, one or the other or both of these characteristic Western distortions of the true picture of world history are likely to persist for some time and to die hard. Nevertheless, it is already possible to look forward to a time when these Western distortions of the true picture, and all other distortions of the kind, will be replaced by a new vision of the past seen from the stand-point, not of this or that nationality, civilization, or religion, but of a united human race.[38]

This sort of thing leads to Toynbee's getting criticized on two counts: he is accused of being too Greek on the one hand and then accused of being too world-minded on the other. The following is the pointed charge of Wilhelmsen, who sees Toynbee as "preparing the way for the assault on the citadel of the West by inviting all of us to view history from the universal point of view."[39] Rather than seeing this as a defect in Toynbee, I should think this may well prove his lasting contribution.

In *Reconsiderations,* Toynbee both defends his Hellenic bias and graciously admits its possible limitations. He views his Hellenic model as "the normal heuristic use of an hypothesis" and on this basis he concludes that he does not think that his practice needs reconsideration or revision. The use of the Hellenic model has "vindicated itself," and after reexamination it appears "that I have not gone astray in employing the model up to its full capacity." We do find some qualifications. "Though this particular key has opened many doors, it has not proved omnicompetent,"[40] he admits. We need other keys: "The Hellenic Civilization is a key that will not unlock all doors, and other tools can and should be used as alternatives where the Hellenic tool fails to do the job."[41] Toynbee confesses that he "overworked this model" and that he "neglected to try other keys where the Hellenic key has obviously not fitted the lock."

Our Hellenic-oriented Englishman does accept one unfortunate effect of his classical education. It has resulted in an unfortunate style: "I often fall into writing English clumsily." He holds that his distaste for French and English is the result of "a classical scholar's irrational prejudice." He is sorry: "I should feel more at home if Greek and Latin were the media of communication between me and my public."[42]

Reconsiderations continues the habit of defending the pattern of including the Roman under the Hellenic, a source of irritation to some of the critics of *A Study.* "There was never any such thing as a self-contained Roman society and civilization," states Toynbee; "to try to divorce Rome from Hellenism and to treat Rome as an independent historical entity would make nonsense of Roman history by placing it in an historical vacuum."[43] When it comes to Rome, Toynbee looks back to Greece: "The outstanding event in Rome's history is Rome's absorption by Hellenism, not the Hellenization of barbarian Western Europe by Rome." Toynbee gives this evaluation of his own point of view: "In calling Rome 'an Hellenic city' he is telling the fundamental truth about her."[44] And again we are reminded that *Hellenic* is a more inclusive word than *Greek* in both a temporal and geographic sense: "The word 'Greek', too, is a misnomer, because in English it suggests the Greek language, and the domains of the Greek language and of Hellenic civilization were never conterminous."[45] The Hellenic civilization included at various times many peoples who never spoke the Greek tongue. Toynbee had a classical education in England and this means a Hellenic education; for this we may be grateful for some rare insights and for some troublesome prejudices perhaps.

Isaiah Berlin tells us that "historical sense is the knowledge not of what happened, but what did not happen."[46] If we accept this criterion, then it would seem to follow that Toynbee's Hellenic orientation has proved a happy one. Toynbee has a fabulous *if* erudition: if this had happened rather than that, if a Chinese education rather than a classical English education, if born then instead of now. To build up an array of *if* possibilities, to have this knowledge of what did not come to pass, an early civilization as a model has certain rather obvious advantages. There must be an intervening sequence of events to permit an accumulation of historical *if*'s. Further, this model must be variously and widely known in the present. On this basis, the Hellenic model seems a happy choice.

Another criterion of the historian's skill from Berlin is the "imaginative projection of ourselves into the past." Again it would appear that the Hellenic model is a happy choice. Toynbee says his generation is the last in England to receive this classical education. For a Western historian, Athens and Rome are rather obvious selections of a past. Toynbee's facility in Greek and Latin, his comfortable at-homeness in them, would certainly pave the way for an "imaginative projection" into the past. If we may trust Whitehead, Toynbee, and others, this continuity with a classical past, this classical erudition, is pretty well gone. The historian with anything approaching Toynbee's classical scholarship is going to be an increasingly rare bird. He may, in fact, be already extinct. So let us thank Toynbee for his effort. He has preserved the Hellenic bias into the twentieth century, perhaps rather too voluminously.

Kenneth Keniston suggests some criteria for the historian which seem to me appropriate in our present discussion of the author of *A Study of History:* ". . .those who seek to maintain the continuity of a tradition must, paradoxically, assume a creative role. We need not only a rediscovery of the vital ideals of the past, but a willingness to create new ideals."[47] On this score it does seem that Toynbee is worthy of our deep gratitude. He has played a "creative and innovating role." His attack on nationalism, his plea for a world state, his hope for a universal past—these and much more are sincere and eloquent. His quarrel with self-centeredness, with parochialism in religion, suggests "new ideals."

IV

Some have held that Toynbee is so Hellenic that he is indifferent and ignorant of the West of his own time. "I am ruefully aware that my classical education has left me almost entirely ignorant of modern Western discoveries, from the seventeenth century onwards, in the fields of mathematics and physical science,"[48] he says. He acknowledges this as "a big blank." Whatever may be this blank and however big it may be, it seems to me that Toynbee has been able to show great insight into the West, and then with this insight to go on and make profound comments about the world at large. I would suggest that his Reith Lectures, *The World and the West* (1952), supply ample evidence of this. However, whatever Toynbee may lack, he does have an Olympian view.

Toynbee, a Westerner and an English Westerner, is not taken in by the West. His approach is ecumenical. For this reason there are those who think of him as a non-Westerner, or even as an anti-Westerner. He assures us in one of his many extensive footnotes that he is not anti-West:

I have a substantial stake in the West's future: eleven grandchildren. How could it be supposed that I am licking my lips over the possibility that they may be wiped out of existence? There is nothing that I want more than that the West should survive. But, to survive, it must save itself. And I believe that irreverence such as mine is the most salutary attitude for Westerners to take towards their civilization in its present crisis. For the last two or three centuries the West has been enjoying an ascendancy over the non-Western majority of mankind. In our time this abnormal and unwholesome position of ours has become untenable. Our problem is how to climb down to a normal level of equality without having a great fall. [49]

The substantial stake of eleven grandchildren, however, does not make Toynbee parochial and nationalistic in his concerns. A good Westerner is no longer an apologist for the West; he must look at the West from a broader base, and this is precisely what Toynbee does and does perhaps better than any one in the field today. On the whole, the West has been just plain lucky, says Toynbee. "Yet the West has been singular, and fortunate, in having been free to move at its own pace. No outsiders have been setting its pace for it."[50] On the other hand, the West has been setting the pace for most of the rest of the world. Here we may think of the efforts of the newly organized states in Asia and Africa. They are undergoing a forced march to try to catch up with the West, and it is not easy.

The West's eminence may be traced to an "unprecedented technological advance" which has given the West "an ascendancy over the rest of mankind." This may be "no more than a temporary episode" in the World's history. Indeed, the general dominance seems already gone: "By the year 1961 the West's former ascendancy was manifestly passing away."[51] Technology had brought the West to this position, but technology was not, and is not, sufficient to keep it on top.

The trouble is that the West has not been morally equal to its technology: ". . .the modern Western civilization has displayed not only a bright side but a dark one, and . . . in our time this dark side has been darker than the darkest on the pages of Western history in the Middle Ages."[52] The West is challenged from within by its nuclear warfare potential with its power to wipe out the human race. Externally there is the challenge of Russia and China. Both of these countries—Russia in particular—have armed themselves with Western technology and with a Western ideology, namely, communism. Toynbee declares, "The Russians and Chinese would never have invented Communism for themselves."[53] In *The World and the West* Toynbee is eloquent in showing how aggression from West to East has gone on for centuries and how now this flow of aggression has reversed itself and goes today from East to West.

With this Western spiritual weapon in her hands, Russia could carry her war with the West into the enemy's country on the spiritual plane. Since Communism had originated as a product of uneasy Western consciences, it could appeal to other uneasy Western consciences when it was radiated back into the Western world by a Russian propaganda.[54]

This circumstance is of special significance to Toynbee because it means that in the current encounter between the world and the West the battle is "moving off the technological plane on to the spiritual plane." On this level the West cannot be so self-assured about its superiority.

Toynbee treats this theme at some length in *Reconsiderations*, and it seems appropriate to quote from that discussion at some length:

A discussion in 1961 of the history and prospects of the West would have been left hanging in the air if it had not been followed up by a discussion of Russia's place in history. Since . . . 1917, Russia has been challenging the West as it has not been challenged since the recession of the Ottoman Islamic power after the failure of the second Ottoman siege of Vienna in 1683. . . . Under Russian leadership, Communism has set out to compete with Liberalism for the adherence of the non-Western majority of mankind. . . . Before 1917 the West was winning converts all over the World to the ideology of the seventeenth-century Western spiritual revolution. Since 1917 the West has been on the defensive against an ideological counter-offensive. . . . Considering how overwhelming the West's ascendancy over most of the rest of the World had been during the preceding quarter of a millennium, Communist Russia's feat of turning the tables on the West was impressive.[55]

Toynbee would assign a dual role to Russia in contemporary history. In one capacity she serves "as the leader in a world-wide resistance movement to the modern West's world-wide aggression."[56] And secondly: "Perhaps Russia's most important role in this next chapter of mankind's history would be to serve as a medium for the modernization of non-Western peoples that Russia herself was."[57] C. P. Snow and Robert Heilbroner both share Toynbee's view on this second role for Russia.[58]

From his vantage point on a historical Olympus, Toynbee looks down on the cold war, the East versus West conflict, as something which will pass away: "The ideological feud that in 1961 was obsessing nearly half the human race might have become no more than an academic issue in the life of an oecumenical society a hundred years later."[59]

At this point there must be many who would lash out at Toynbee and damn his thinking as the work of a man who is in love with the ecumenical, one whose perspective is so wide that he fails to see the dangers of his own era; after all one does live and die in his own day. Here we have this mortician of civilizations daring to refer to our East-West conflict as a passing academic issue. Is this just another Toynbeean extravagance? Mutual fear must be replaced with mutual love. In an atomic world, "the standard of conduct demanded from ordinary human beings can be no lower than the standard attained in times past by rare saints."[60]

Toynbee may seem extreme to some of the hard realists in cold-war strategy. But he is not alone; he is not alone in many of his observations. For example, a group of economists write: "In our times it is no longer the specter of Communism which is haunting Europe, but rather emerging industrialization that is confronting the whole world."[61] The ideological conflict is no longer so critical. "The age of ideology fades. . . . The age of utopias is past. An age of realism has taken its place; an age in which there is little expectation of either utter perfection or complete doom."[62] Of course, these economists and Toynbee are not using the same language, nor are they in agreement on what is central. My point is this: there is a shifting of the ground. What was relevant may no longer be so.

Erich Fromm's conclusion in *May Men Prevail?* has a good deal in common with the above comments. Industrialism, technology, etc., have been moving and pushing both the USSR and the USA in pretty much the same direction. The two great antagonists of this period of history are becoming more and more alike. This may not make for very effective propaganda stories, but it does have something to do with long-term trends.

We have first to overcome the hysterical and irrational concepts Russians and Americans have about each other. As Fromm sees it, the USSR is "a conservative, totalitarian, managerialism, and not a revolutionary system with the aim of world domination." And to him, the US is "no longer a capitalistic system of individual initiative, free competition." Both are bureaucratic industrial societies. [63]

On this issue and many others I would take the position that reading Toynbee can be an inspiration for the long pull, for the unparochial view. The trouble may be that we have too many who do not want to look very far ahead. Toynbee may help to increase their number. This influence, I would hold, is one of his major contributions to contemporary thought.

V

Some have taken it on faith or otherwise that God chose the Jewish people as the vehicle for making known His purposes for men everywhere. Toynbee does not see it this way. Rather than God making the selection, the Jews themselves decided that they were God's chosen people: "The Jews have told their own story from the standpoint of a self-proclaimed 'Chosen People,' "[64] It is Toynbee's treatment of Jews which has led to the most violent reactions to *A Study of History*. The final section of volume XII is entitled "Reconsiderations of Particular Topics." Chapter headings read as follows:

Explanations and Revisions of Usages of Terms.
The Relation between Man and His Environment.
The Transitional Societies.
Originality versus Mimesis.
The Configuration of Middle American and Andean History.
Rome's Place in History.
The Configuration of Syriac History.
Islam's Place in History.
The History and Prospects of the Jews.
The History and Prospects of the West.
Russia's Place in History.
A Re-survey of Civilizations.
The Next Ledge.

Each of these—other than the last—has been the subject of controversy and heated adverse criticism. Four of them seem to me to stand out with particular urgency. They are Islam, the Jews, the West, and Russia. Ten pages are devoted to Islam and Russia. The chapter on the West rates eighteen pages. But the reconsideration of the history and prospects of the Jews takes forty-one pages. Toynbee tells us that it is more profitable to learn from one's critics than to fight them. Toynbee is a kindly man and a willing man. As one critic puts it, "One is compelled to admire Toynbee's willingness to scrap much of his own work in favor of fresh ideas and new approaches."[65]

Well, does our historian back away from the hornets' nest he created throughout literally thousands of pages in *A Study* by his treatment of the Jews? Does he hedge? Does he shift to less disputed themes? Scarcely, or very little at any rate, if at all. Again in volume XII as in the original work, comments on the Jews are scattered throughout.

To Toynbee, the great sin as well as the original sin is self-centeredness. And he finds the Jews self-centered: "Self-centredness is perhaps even more difficult to cope with in its plural form than it is in the singular, because it is both more insidious and more potent."[66]

Toynbee's case against the Jews—if one may use the word *against* in this sense—takes place on several levels.

1. The Jews continue to think of themselves as the chosen people. "I reject the pretension to be 'a Chosen People' in whatever people's name it is made,"[67] Toynbee declares.

2. "On reconsideration, I do not find that I have changed my view of Zionism,"[68] he says again. It is an example of nationalism and colonialism.

3. "From A.D. 135 to A.D. 1948 there was no such thing as a Jewish state, and not even such a thing as a Jewish 'national home' . . ." writes Toynbee. Many have tried to make much of the way the Jewish people preserved a sense of people and state in such a long period of diaspora. Toynbee is not overly impressed: "This fact is remarkable and exceptional, but it is not unique. The Jews are not the only people who have achieved it."[69]

4. The thing which really upsets the Jewish people is Toynbee's insistence on calling their religion a *fossil* religion: ". . .Jewish critics have attacked me for my use of the word 'fossil' as if I had applied it to the Jews alone, and applied it to them as a term of abuse. . . ."[70] Upon reconsideration we have: "I do hold that Judaism, as well as Jewry, is a fossil both of the Syriac Civilization and of Syriac religion."[71] But this is not quite the final word: "I have now admitted that the word 'fossil' describes only partially and inadequately what I mean by it. But it does ex-

press important parts of my meaning, and I still have not found an apter word to replace it."[72] If some one could supply him with a better label, he would adopt this "golden word with alacrity."

5. Toynbee is a bit rough on the Jewish god Yahweh. He calls him a "well-known barbaric type" and states that "this primitive Yahweh is worse than vindictive; he is moody, capricious, and impulsive. Many of his acts are so arbitrary as to be unaccountable."[73]

6. He is annoyed at the Jewish possessiveness in the case of their religion: "Christianity and Islam each quickly rid itself of the handicap of being a Jewish national religion and an Arab national religion respectively, whereas Judaism has never ceased to be a Jewish national religion. . . ."[74]

Perhaps some of the sting is removed when in the closing pages Toynbee admits to "three dim spots and one general short-coming":

1. "my neglect of the civilization in which I myself have been brought up."

2. "my neglect of Israel, Judah, the Jews, and Judaism. I have neglected these out of proportion to their true importance."

3. "my third dim spot in my study of civilizations is South-East Asia, continental and insular."

4. "the general shortcoming . . . is [that] . . . I have taken too little note of some of the threads that weave the ever-changing pattern of a culture. . . ."[75]

While Toynbee does not seem to alter his position on Jews and their religion, he does list his neglect of their contribution as one of the four major shortcomings in his study of civilizations.

It is not only Jews who have objected to Toynbee's treatment of the Jews. The Protestant weekly *The Christian Century* felt obligated to take him to task for his comments on Judaism:

The Jews, according to Toynbee, have a mission in the world, but it is a mission borne best by a progressive loss of identity, an eventual fusion of Jewish life and thought into the coming Great Religion. . . . But it is always ungracious for the "outsider" to wish non-being on a group having a valid religious heritage. Time, not Toynbee, will bring the eroding winds.[76]

Let us now turn to a Jewish critic—Rabbi Jacob B. Agus —whom Toynbee describes in these words: "no critic could be more temperate and objective-minded than he is." Agus finds three sore spots for Jewish people in the writings of Toynbee: (1) "his characterization of the Jewish people as a fossil of Syriac civilization"; (2) "Judaic zealotry"; and (3) "his bitter condemnation of the Zionist movement and the State of Israel."[77]

While Agus recognizes these three things as bitter pills for the Jewish people, he also feels that the Jewish people have some very important things to learn from Toynbee and his works:

What is it then—now that the dust of passion and resentment stirred up among Jews by Toynbee's work is happily beginning to settle—that the Jewish community has to learn from this volume and its author. Seeing oneself in the perspective of world history entails, particularly for Jews, a good deal more than finding an occasion for self-gratulation on the crucial role one has played in it. Above all, it entails the obligation to understand one's involvement in the general condition. Such an obligation is especially salutary for Jews, who tend, because their history has been unparalleled, to believe that they have been permanently exempted from the laws of history.[78]

Agus holds that sensitive Jews "have an almost aching need to see the Jewish people in the perspective of world history. Perhaps that is the reason they fastened so intently onto Toynbee's work."[79] In regard to Zionism and Israel, we have this from Agus: ". . . and it is this lesson (not to form a tight closed society in Israel) above all that one carries away from a consideration of Toynbee's new epistle to the Jews."[80]

Agus, a Jew, sees the need for Toynbee's world perspective. Can one think of any particular religion, any particular nation, and, if you will, any particular discipline which could not profit also from this corrective?

VI

Reconsiderations adds to the already too monumental *A Study of History*. But volume XII is also a monument in its own right. No other author has ever seen himself so frequently dissected and the focus of attention on the part of such a variety of surgeons. Toynbee seems more than willing to talk to each one in his turn. Each one of them may be dismissed in the end, but one would search long and hard for a hurried, premature, petulant dismissal. No one seems to be beneath his notice. It must be said to Toynbee's credit that he did not pad *Reconsiderations* with the

flattering words of his eulogists and his apologists. He could very
easily have made this book into an encyclopedic cover-jacket
plug. He does not. He brings in the harshest, the bitterest, the
most penetrating comments: "The whole concept of
Reconsiderations is fantastic. In keeping with the magnitude of
the *Study,* there are 700 closely packed pages given to second
thoughts and to an examination of every known opinion of the
author's original work."[81]

And what is the result? Essentially what we have is more of
Toynbee. For all the prodigious reconsidering, not much is
changed: a slight shift here and a hesitant qualification there.

In the end, the critics can hardly rejoice over the corrections
Toynbee makes in *Reconsiderations.* He admits his error in thinking that man went from the Upper Palaeolithic hunter's way of
life to civilization at a single bound. In fact, this transition took
two steps. He admits, too, that in the light of new knowledge he
has had to give up his notion that Central America had three dis-
tinct civilizations. There was just one.

There is this profound concession to his historian adversaries:
"On reconsideration, I now think that I over-estimated the importance of the Minoan-Helladic-Mycenaean contribution to the
civilization or civilizations that arose in Syria towards the end of
the second millennium B.C."[82] While he has revised his original
picture of Syriac history considerably, he nevertheless warns us,
"I shall not be surprised if my second picture is criticized as vig-
orously as my first has been," but he hopes that all this effort at
reconsideration "may at least help to elucidate a passage of history which is as important as it is enigmatic."[83] And we have this
well-qualified reconsideration: "On reconsideration, then, I agree
that force has sometimes played a decisive part in human
affairs."[84]

Toynbee revises his list of civilizations. This is, of course, the
major reconsideration. But what is the result? Here and there a
specialist—a type of scholar that Toynbee does not care for in the
first place—will cry out Eureka over this revision. But who can
keep in mind the full range of these civilizations—who can hang
on to this Toynbeean erudition long enough—to get the full impact of this revised chart of civilizations?

It is somewhat easier to catch the revisions Toynbee proposes
in the usages of terms. For example, he says, "The notion of
withdrawal-and-return has been perhaps more sharply criticized

than any other idea of mine, and, on reconsideration, I am inclined to think that I have put more weight on it than it will bear."[85] Further, he adds, "On reconsideration, I think that, in previous volumes, I have painted the contrast between the 'creative' and the 'dominant' phase in the rule of a minority in too strong colors."[86] Also a third example: "I have tended to oversimplify, and hence to exaggerate, the contrast between original creation and 'mimesis.'. . . ."[87]

I have a few reservations about the first ten volumes, and I cannot say that I am any the happier about these reservations as a result of *Reconsiderations*. If Toynbee may use the Hellenic "model" for heuristic purposes, if he may use "analogy" for heuristic purposes, then I plead guilty of using Toynbee for heuristic purposes; and I am quite happy in so doing. I am not a historian, so it is easy for me to accept Toynbee on these terms. I love Toynbee when I read him on my own terms. I can accept the anonymous review in *Time:* ". . .with all its errors of detail, the *History* was the boldest and most exciting effort yet made by a modern historian to chart man's troubled, inspired climb from primitive morass to a fellowship of man and God." I find the following in the same review a bit too extreme: "Toynbee lacerates himself too much, and the total effect is damaging."[88] *Reconsiderations* did not damage *A Study of History*, as I see it.

Geoffrey Bruun feels that Toynbee's "ambitious interpretation is still an unproven hypothesis, quite possibly a mistaken hypothesis." Even so, his contribution is enormous. Toynbee has done "more than any other living thinker to redress the balance between the microscopic view of history and the panoramic view of it."[89] Moody, too, has kind words for our historian. He says Toynbee belongs in the line of Augustine, Vico, Marx, and Spengler. His imagination is equal to theirs and his scholarship is superior. It is Toynbee who has had the courage to break down the conventional boundaries of the specialists. "To a significant degree Toynbee has thus helped to form the intellectual history of our time,"[90] declares J. N. Moody.

With the passage of time *A Study of History* has come to be seen as an unbelievable achievement of virtuosity and persistence; in truth it is one of the wonders of the scholarly world. Many thinkers from diverse disciplines have had their say about *A Study*. Surely this vast work is deserving of the compendium of commentaries Toynbee has deemed fit to assemble in

Reconsiderations. Without this final volume Toynbee would not have been Toynbee, and *A Study of History* would itself have been incomplete.

CHAPTER 6

Religious Historian, Agnostic Man

IN the eighteenth century Edward Gibbon boldly declared in *The Decline and Fall of the Roman Empire* that it was Christianity which had destroyed Greek civilization. Later in his autobiography he was to comment: "Had I believed that the majority of English readers were so fondly attached even to the name and shadow of Christianity; had I foreseen that the pious, the timid, and the prudent would feel or affect to feel, with such sensibility; I might, perhaps, have softened the two invidious chapters which would create many enemies, and conciliate few friends."

However, "the shaft was shot, the alarm was sounded, and I could only rejoice that, if the voice of our priests was clamorous and bitter, their hands were disarmed from the powers of persecution."[1]

For some time now readers of *A Study of History* might have anticipated Arnold J. Toynbee writing in an introspective, penitent mood not unlike that of Gibbon something on this order: Had I believed that the majority of Western historians were so fondly attached even to the name and shadow of enmity toward Christianity; had I foreseen that the scientific and historical scholar would feel or affect to feel with such exquisite sensibility; I might perhaps have softened my conclusion that religion is the essence of history, a thesis which would create many enemies among historians and conciliate few religious friends. But the shaft was shot, the alarm sounded; and I could only rejoice that, if the voice of our historians was clamorous and bitter, their hands were disarmed from the powers of persecution.

Toynbee has yet to pen this second thought. While he has softened many of the positions taken in *A Study of History*, he has yet to come up with this Gibbonian reflection. What is more, we have reason to believe that Toynbee's autobiography is now complete. We had *Reconsiderations* in 1961; *Acquaintances* in 1967; and *Experiences* in 1969. "I am now over eighty years old. Have I not discharged my obligation? Am I not now at liberty to bow myself out. . . . My expectation of life is now short."[2] We have good reason, then, to believe that the autobiographical statement has been given, and while Toynbee has softened his remarks on Jews as God's chosen people, he has not as a historian softened his thesis of religion in history.

Toynbee has specifically responded to his differences with Gibbon: Christianity could not have destroyed Greek civilization for that civilization had been in a state of decay well in advance of the rise of Christianity. Christianity, rather than being a destroyer of civilization, serves as a chrysalis from which a civilization may grow. This, Toynbee would have us believe, is "an alternative to the theory of Christianity being the destroyer of the ancient Graeco-Roman civilization."[3]

Christianity becomes the egg, grub, and chrysalis "between butterfly and butterfly." At this point, we need not pursue the thesis of religion as a chrysalis for civilization. Our purpose is the simple one of showing a certain reverse parallelism between Gibbon and Toynbee.

We can be quite blunt: in this century, Toynbee is *the religious historian*. This is not to say he is the historian of religions, which would be quite another matter. *A Study of History* is viewed by some as this century's equivalent of Augustine's *City of God*. Toynbee is variously seen as prophet and theologian. He has been called the Billy Graham of the intelligentsia. H. J. Muller has attacked him as an arrogant religionist. He resents Toynbee's assumption that only a return to God can save civilization; the "arrogant assumption that Christianity is the apex of spiritual progress."[4] As Muller sees it, Toynbee's work eventuates in the conclusion that religion is the whole meaning and end of history. As an historian, Muller believes that Toynbee is obsessed with religion.

Walter Kaufmann likens Toynbee's religiousness to a Hollywood production: it is spectacular and has a huge cast.[5] Christopher Dawson sees our historian as making enemies on all sides. His reduction of history to theology "will not meet with any more favor from the theologian and the students of comparative religion, than it has done from the historians."[6]

One could with ease extend the inventory of unfavorable comments on Toynbee's religious bias. In the eye of the historian and the theologian he is seen as the religious historian. This is his reputation in the annals of scholarship.

Toynbee does all sorts of things, large and small, to justify this view. For example, he writes: "the longer the writer of this *Study* lived, the more glad he was that he had been born early enough in the Western Civilization's day to have been taken to church as a child every Sunday as a matter of course."[7] And he could write—in dead seriousness we suspect:

> The African Negritos are said by our anthropologists to have an unexpectedly pure and lofty conception of the nature of God and of God's relation to man. They might be able to give man a fresh start; and, though we should have lost the achievements of the last 6,000 to 10,000 years, what are 10,000 years as compared to the 600,000 or a million years for which the human race has already been in existence. The extreme possibility of catastrophe is that we might succeed in exterminating the whole human race, African Negritos and all.[8]

What is more, his religious erudition is nothing short of astounding. Reading *A Study* leaves one with the impression that here is a man who has quite literally memorized The Bible and who moves with scholarly ease in the major and minor religions of the world. One has the feeling that Toynbee would be at home in an obscure commentary on a minor Asian faith or the ritualistic details of an African supplicatory dance. The erudition is fantastic and the asides innumerable.

If we would understand *A Study of History*, two concepts seem essential from the very start: higher religions and the evolution of the religious impulse. Toynbee states:

> By higher religions I mean religions designed to bring human beings into direct communion with absolute spiritual Reality as individuals, in contrast to earlier forms of religion that have brought them only into indirect communion with It through the medium of the particular society in which they have happened to be participants. Religion, in these earlier forms, is an integral part of the culture of some particular society. On the other hand the higher religions have broken—some partially, some

completely—out of the configuration of the particular cultures in which
they originated. They have become separate systems of specifically religious culture, in a state of tension with the systems of secular culture
with which they have parted company.[9]

There is a set progression which culminates in a higher religion.
We have this progress: (1) nature-worship; (2) man-worship,
which may take the form of nationalism, communism, or individualism; (3) "direct personal touch with the ultimate spiritual
reality behind all the phenomena of the Universe, non-human
and human alike."[10] This last is higher religion: "A religion earns
the title 'higher' in virtue of its being an attempt to bring human
souls into direct touch with the ultimate spiritual presence behind the phenomena of the Universe."[11] It is higher because it
has risen above man-worship and nature-worship. We are approx-
imating here in one way or another some of Chardin's religious
evolution and something of Tillich's God above God.

History, too, is a progression; it is "a vision of God's creation
on the move, from God its source toward God its goal."[12] God is
what motivates man in history. The ability of man to climb toward "an unattained and invisible ledge above . . . was going to
be decided by the course of Man's relations, not just with his fellow men and with himself, but, above all, with God his Savior."[13]

Once history is seen as movement from God as source to God
as goal, we can then arrange history in a progression of stages: (1)
primitive societies; (2) primary civilizations; (3) secondary civilizations, and (4) higher religions.

We have civilizations in order that we may have higher religions, declares Toynbee:

If this view of the prospects of Religion were to carry conviction, it
would open up a new view of the role of the civilizations. If the movement of the chariot of Religion was continuous in its rise and constant in
its direction, the cyclic and recurrent movement of the rises and falls of
civilizations might be not only antithetical but subordinate. It might, as
we have surmised, serve its purpose, and find its significance, in promoting the fiery chariot's ascent towards Heaven by periodic revolutions on
Earth of "the sorrowful wheel" of birth-death-birth. In this perspective
the civilizations of the first and second generations might justify their existence, but those of the third generation would cut a disconcertingly
poor figure. If civilizations were the handmaids of Religion, and if the
Hellenic Civilization had served as a good handmaid to Christianity by

bringing this higher religion to birth before that civilization had finally fallen to pieces, then the civilizations of the third generation would appear to be "vain repetitions" of the heathen.[14]

Civilizations fulfill their function "once they [have] brought mature higher religions to birth."

The above statement reflects Toynbee's position from volume VII onward through the remaining volumes of *A Study*. We have remarked how, in volume VII, we get what we may call the great switch in Toynbee. For six big volumes and for some twenty studious years his thesis had been that civilization constituted an intelligible unit for historical study. Nations and empires were insufficient units. In volume VII civilizations, too, go out as a worthy unit of study. Without any real warning, he says: "we have once more drawn a blank. If we are to continue our investigation, we must make a fresh start from quite a different premise."[15]

That different premise and new start is announced on the very next page: "let us try the effect of reversing our point of view. Let us open our minds to the possibility that . . . the histories of the civilizations might have to be envisaged and interpreted in terms, not of their own destinies, but of their effect on the history of religion." This is what Toynbee calls "our new experimental procedure of viewing the histories of civilizations in terms of the histories of higher religions." On the basis of this experimental procedure, the first thing we must do is "to revise our previous tacit and uncritical assumptions about the *raison d'être* of civilization." Henceforth we are to assume that the purpose of civilization is to provide "an opportunity for the fully-fledged higher religions to come to birth."[16]

With this dispatch Toynbee lets us know that civilizations as well as what he calls "parochial states" have ceased to be intelligible fields of study for historians and have "forfeited their historical significance except in so far as they minister to the progress of Religion." We have now achieved what he holds to be "this more illuminating standpoint." This is rather extreme stuff, but Toynbee goes even further: from now on "the birth of a civilization is a catastrophe if it is a regression from a previously established church, while the breakdown of a civilization is not a catastrophe if it is the overture to a church's birth."[17]

A church or a religion is the work of an "internal

proletariat"—the people who live within an empire but are not part of it. It is within this group that we find "sparks of life" and "germs of creative power" which prevent a complete collapse and which allow some continuity from one civilization to another. Out of the internal proletariat comes the chrysalis which permits a civilization to go on to a higher level. Toynbee further sees the capital cities of the world as having had their "historic mission" by becoming centers for the dissemination of religious currents.

Higher religion thus becomes the goal of civilization as well as the impulse which propels the progress of civilizations (or men). This is God as revelation through history and history as the revelation of God. Nationalism, geography, and economics are pushed aside as historic explanations. Higher religion becomes a kind of guiding motif in history; indeed, higher religion is history. And this is what we have in mind when we say that Toynbee is the religious historian.

There are further dimensions to Toynbee as the religious historian. He identifies six higher religions: Zoroastrianism, Judaism, Buddhism, Hinduism, Christianity, and Islam. In his less permissive moments, these six get reduced to four primary religions with Zoroastrianism and Judaism farther off to the side in limbo. These four turn out to be coincident with Carl Jung's psychology. Jung has two basic attitudes, introversion and extraversion, and four basic functions, thinking, feeling, sensation, and intuition. Out of these two attitudes and four functions we come up with four basic human personality types: an introvert with a bias toward thinking; an introvert with an intuitive bent; an extravert with a tendency toward sensation; and an extravert with a strong disposition toward love.

We add Jung to Toynbee, and lo and behold we arrive at a synthesis of higher religions and human personality types, which correspond with these higher religions; and all of this becomes history in the Toynbeean frame of reference. The patterning becomes very neat. Two religions are Indic in origin: Hinduism and Buddhism. These two are the introvert pair with Hinduism displaying the thinking bias and Buddhism the intuitive bias. Two religions are Judaic in origin: Christianity and Islam. These two are the extravert pair with Christianity indicating a love bias and Islam a sensation bias.

This is one dependency of Toynbee, the religious historian, on Jung, the religious psychologist. A further Jungian dimension in

A *Study of History* is the concept of primordial images: "The primordial image is a mnemonic deposit, an imprint which has arisen through a condensation of innumerable, similar processes. It is primarily a precipitate or deposit . . . a certain ever-recurring psychic experience."[18] Primordial images constitute what has been variously called the collective unconscious, the unconscious psyche, psychic depths, or psychic well-spring. Jung's position allows Toynbee to bring the Greek and the modern together—a habit which is especially congenial to Toynbee's way of thinking. He likes to carry his classicism around in a modern psychological Jungian basket:

> It is true that even the fathers of Hellenic philosophy were not so thoroughly blinded by the dazzling light of a newly discovered Reason as to be altogether without an inkling of an irrational psychic life brewing below this brightly illuminated surface of the Psyche in the dark deeps of a subconscious abyss. Aristotle perceived and declared that "the Intellect by itself moves nothing"; and Plato had anticipated, and advanced beyond, this merely negative Aristotelian dictum in his myth of the Soul as a charioteer driving two mettlesome steeds of diverse temperaments. At the same time, it was left to the children of a Western Civilization . . . to follow up these Hellenic surmises by tardily embarking on the scientific exploration of a psychic underworld that had been familiar to Indic and Sinic contemporaries of the Hellenic discoverers of the Intellect. . . .[19]

It is Jung who is outstanding in updating these glimpses enjoyed in the distant past. It is this aspect of Jungian psychology which Toynbee taps so frequently.

The spiritual occupies a major place in much of Toynbee's history. These spiritual forces come not from the intellect of man but from the racial collective psyche. The subconscious, not the intellect, is the "organ through which Man lives his spiritual life for good or evil. It is the fount of Poetry, Music, and the Visual Arts, and the channel through which the Soul is in communion with God when it does not steel itself against God's influence." If we could only "strike rock-bottom in the psychic cosmos," we would gain a "fuller vision of God the Dweller in the Innermost."[20] It is the church which can best handle this psychic energy, the psychic storms which take place when a civilization is in the process of decay.

This, then, in brief, is Toynbee, the religious historian. He is glad he went to church as a boy. He is overwhelming in his religious erudition. But more importantly, Toynbee views history as the process which culminates in higher religions. History, to him, is the movement from God as source to God as goal. Further, these same higher religions that are the final products of civilization correspond to Jung's basic human personality types. And finally, the collective unconscious is man's pipeline to God, is man's inspiration for art and poetry. In *Acquaintances*, which is more autobiographical than historical, one may read: "The greatest souls within our knowledge are the prophets and preachers of the higher religions. . . . Religion is the field in which greatness has proved to have the widest range of action, in both time and space."[21]

One has no hesitation in asserting that Toynbee is the religious historian, but one experiences a manifest reservation in describing Toynbee as a religious person in any of the usual meanings we associate with this term.[22] I am well aware that there is a certain danger in stating that a man is one thing in his profession and quite another thing in his person. Yet in Toynbee's case, I think we can safely refer to him as the religious historian and the agnostic man. These designations need not be taken to suggest a weakening of Toynbee's conviction as an historian nor of doubting his sincerity as a man. We are not engaging in paradox. Nor is it a situation in which our historian so broadly and generously defines religion that he as an agnostic can take shelter under a definitionally all-inclusive umbrella.

In Toynbee: history is the movement from God the source to God the goal.

In Toynbee: religion is man's "relation to an ultimate reality behind and beyond the phenomena of the Universe in which each of us awakens to consciousness."

He means to say both of these things.

We have looked in a most limited way—a full examination would require volumes—at the religious historian. We now turn to the person.

It is as a person living in the twentieth century, rather than as a mortician of civilizations, that Toynbee notes a decline in religion. It is, as it were, at low ebb.

Men have shifted their allegiance from religion to science; and this shift has had the effect of undermining "the intellectual foundations of traditional religion." A further discrediting of religion can be traced to the Western wars of religion. These factors together have brought "religious belief to a perhaps unprecedentedly low ebb":[23]

Meanwhile, this weakening of Christianity's hold on Western hearts was bound to lead these hearts to transfer their devotion to non-Christian objects of worship. This was bound to happen if it is true that religion is one of the stable ingredients in human nature. Human nature, like the rest of nature, abhors a vacuum; and therefore, the devotion that, in human hearts, has been progressively withdrawn from Christianity in the course of the last three centuries has had to find substitutes for Christianity to which it can transfer itself. The substitutes that it has found are the post-Christian ideologies. The three principal representatives of these are Nationalism, Individualism, and Communism, and, of these three, Nationalism is the most obsessive.[24]

In *Experiences*, where Toynbee is both "the subject as well as the narrator," we find Toynbee referring over and over to himself as an ex-Christian, as an ex-believer, and, with greatest frequency, as an agnostic. As an ex-Christian agnostic he says he is "a typical agnostic of my generation in the Western World." He continues: "In the Western Christendom during the last three hundred years there has been progressive falling-away from belief in traditional Christian doctrine. An example of this is my own recession from Christian orthodoxy to agnosticism."[25]

It does not seem right, I know, but one of the best statements Toynbee has made on his present belief occurs in a *Playboy* interview; the result is a commentary which gives a good deal of insight into his religious views. We learn that he considers himself very unorthodox from the standpoint of any of the major religions. To him, Christianity is but one of a half dozen ways of looking at the universe. Each one in its own way makes its contribution. Toynbee says he finds something in each one of them, but he "couldn't swallow any one of them whole." He affirms again that his own religious conviction is that of agnosticism. When pressed to define his position, he admits to believing there is a spiritual reality in the cosmos, but this spiritual reality is not a personality as many religions hold. He is agnostic in the sense that he feels we ought to admit our ignorance about basic religious questions. When asked, would he think of himself as a humanist, his quick answer is, "certainly not." He cannot stomach the humanist notion that human beings are the highest form of spiritual existence: "When human beings worship themselves as gods, they always quickly come to grief."[26]

The first clear indication, of which I am aware, that Toynbee considers himself an agnostic occurs in *Reconsiderations* (1961). There he refers to himself as an "ex-believer" in the text and as an "agnostic" in a footnote. In *Experiences* (1969), he is ever so much more open in his agnostic stance: "I know that I should not pass the most elementary tests of Christian orthodoxy." Thus Christianity is out. Judaism is out too, of course. "I do not believe the Jews are God's Chosen People." He cannot accept the Islam position that Muhammad is "the last prophet." As for Buddhism, the transmigration of souls is too much for him to swallow. Zoroastrianism, he declares, "presents perhaps the fewest stumbling blocks to me." However, he cannot accept their belief that warfare between good and evil is destined to end after a season. Hinduism might admit him, but there, in the hierarchy of castes, he feels that he would "rank below the sweepers."[27]

Toynbee became an agnostic while an undergraduate at Oxford. He never could accept the notion that Christ had been born without a human father: "Now more than half a century later, I am still an agnostic."[28]

Our ex-believer would have "the maximum of religion with the minimum of dogma."[29] Love is the avenue for maximizing religion, for love is God. He writes that his creed consists of a single article: "For a human being, God is the act of helping another human being." He adds to this single article the claims that the true end of man is "self-sacrificing love"; that love is divine and that this is "the only god that we know from human experience"; and that man should "devote himself to this god without any reservations, whatever the consequences may be." As human beings we have no experience of God "apart from love,"[30] he declares. "I believe that the dweller in the innermost sanctum of a human being is identical with the spiritual presence behind and beyond the Universe, and I believe that this ultimate spiritual reality is love."[31]

It seems strange to find a historian who holds that the purpose of civilization is to create higher religions, should himself repudiate this or that primary tenet in each of these religions, and end up with the belief that God is love and that dogmas have little or nothing to do with religion. A reading of *A Study of History* scarcely prepares one for this finale. More than anything else it was Toynbee's religious bias in general and his Anglican bias in particular that made him *persona non grata* with his fellow historians.

Still, one would have to admit as one made his way through *A Study* and many of Toynbee's other books that there is an ecumenical and pluralistic permissiveness which points at least indirectly, if not directly, toward this agnosticism. With Toynbee, it has never been one religion. There are many, many religions and there are at least four, if not six, higher religions. Over and over in Toynbee, sin is self-centeredness; sin is the assumption that one is God's chosen.

Toynbee does not expect one religion to be adequate for the variety of men on earth. Nor does he expect a single faith to penetrate the mystery that is ours:

Different people's convictions will differ, because Absolute Reality is a mystery of which no more than a fraction has ever been penetrated by—or been revealed to—any human mind. "The heart of so great a mystery cannot ever be reached by following one road only." However strong and confident may be my conviction that my approach to the mystery is the right one, I ought to be aware that my field of spiritual vision is so narrow that I cannot know that there is no virtue in other approaches.[32]

As soon as we dogmatically hold to one religion and try to force this upon another person or culture, we are in effect placing ourselves between God and a man who would commune with God in his soul's own way. "The missions of the higher religions are not competitive; they are complementary," he avers. We can love our own religion without demanding that it is the "sole means of salvation."[33] Our descendants are "not going to be just Western, like ourselves." They will be the heirs of Confucius, Buddha, Zarathustra, Shankara as well as the heirs of Plato and Aristotle and the Hebrew prophets.

What is one to make of an historian who writes a twelve-volume study of history which holds that civilizations arise from the chrysalis of religious creative minorities and have as their final goal a higher religion; an historian whose religious erudition simply and completely surpasses all others; and then in his final intellectual will and testament proudly announces that he has been an agnostic all along? Here we have an historian who uses religion as the very structure on which to hang his theses and document his postures; and then at eighty he says that his belief consists in one sentence: God is love.

Generally, the historians have damned his religious structuring of history, and the theologians have damned his ex-Christian beliefs. By and large, the secularists have not defended his agnosticism, nor have the religionists applauded his religious approach to history. Toynbee is most commonly praised for religious erudition.

I should praise, admire, cherish Toynbee on two counts: conviction and openness. In some persons these two qualities would suggest a primary conflict. In Toynbee, strangely and happily, they can be complementary attitudes, and thus Toynbee becomes, not just an historian, nor just an agnostic, but one of our day's most engaging personalities.

It is certainly appropriate, then, to call Arnold J. Toynbee a religious historian and an agnostic man, and to do this with the knowledge that we are the richer for both the historian and the man.

Notes and References

Preface

1. Arnold Toynbee, *Between Oxus and Jumna* (New York: Oxford University Press), p. 93.
2. Toynbee, "Comment: A Reply to Geyl and Fiess," *Journal of the History of Ideas* XVI (June, 1955), 421.

Chapter One

1. Christopher Dawson, "Review of *A Study of History*," *International Affairs* Vol. 31 (April, 1955), 155.
2. Georg Hegel, *Lectures on the Philosophy of History* (London: Henry G. Bohn, 1857), pp. 5–6.
3. Walter Kaufmann, "Toynbee and Super-History," *Partisan Review* 22, no. 4 (Fall, 1955), 532.
4. George Catlin, "Toynbee's Study of History," *Political Science Quarterly* 70 (March, 1955), 107.
5. *A Study of History*, I, 4.
6. Sir Ernest Barker, "Review of *A Study of History*," *International Affairs* XXXI (January, 1955), 15.
7. *A Study of History*, I, vii.
8. Toynbee, *Civilization on Trial* and *The World and the West* (Cleveland: Meridian Books, 1958), p. 15.
9. Toynbee, *Experiences* (New York: Oxford University Press, 1969), p. 89.
10. *Ibid.*, p. 91.
11. *A Study of History*, I, 151–52.
12. *Ibid.*, p. 153.
13. *Civilization on Trial*, p. 80.
14. *Ibid.*, p. 85.
15. Toynbee, "*A Study of History:* What I Am Trying to Do," *Diogenes* no. 13 (Spring, 1956), 8.
16. *A Study of History*, I, 9.
17. *Ibid.*, p. 11.
18. *Ibid.*, p. 5.
19. *Ibid.*, pp. 3–4.
20. *Ibid.*, p. 2.

21. *Ibid.*, IX, 205.

22. *Ibid.*, pp. 205–6.

23. *Ibid.*, I, 7.

24. Ernst Cassirer, *An Essay on Man* (Garden City: Doubleday Anchor, 1953), p. 243.

25. *A Study of History*, I, 8.

26. Toynbee, "New Vistas for the Historian," *Saturday Review*, January 7, 1956, p. 64.

27. Toynbee, "*A Study of History:* What I Am Trying To Do," p. 10.

28. *A Study of History*, IX, 215.

29. *Ibid.*, I, 8.

30. *Civilization On Trial*, p. 11.

31. *Ibid.*, p. 143.

32. *A Study of History*, IX, 341.

33. *Civilization on Trial*, p. 195.

34. *A Study of History*, X, 80.

35. F. H. Underhill, "The Toynbee of the 1950s," *The Canadian Historical Review* XXXVI (September, 1955), 230.

36. *A Study of History*, XII, 80.

37. *Civilization on Trial*, p. 33.

38. Dawson, "Toynbee's Study of History," *International Affairs* XXXI (April, 1955), 149.

39. *A Study of History*, X, 95.

40. Toynbee, "*A Study of History:* What I Am Trying to Do," p. 6.

41. *A Study of History*, III, 476.

42. *Ibid.*, VIII, 673.

43. Max Lerner, "American Thought: The Angle of Vision," *American Scholar* 23, no. 3 (Summer, 1954), 265.

44. *A Study of History*, III, 128.

45. *Ibid.*, p. 216.

46. *Ibid.*, p. 233.

47. *Ibid.*, p. 373.

48. *Ibid.*, p. 377.

49. *Ibid.*, IV, 12.

50. *Ibid.*, p. 23.

51. *Ibid.*, p. 115.

52. *Ibid.*, pp. 119–20.

53. *Ibid.*, VII, 53.

54. *Ibid.*, p. 69.

55. *Ibid.*, p. 54.

56. *Ibid.*, IX, 289.

57. *Ibid.*, VII, 420.

58. *Ibid.*, p. 423.

59. *Ibid.*, pp. 425—26.

60. *Ibid.*, X, 1–3.

61. *Ibid.*, p. 42.
62. *Civilization on Trial*, pp. 206–7.
63. *A Study of History*, III, 431.
64. *Civilization on Trial*, p. 44.
65. *A Study of History*, IX, 201.
66. *Ibid.*, pp. 736–37.
67. *Ibid.*, X, 7.
68. *Ibid.*, p. 113.
69. Toynbee, *Acquaintances* (New York: Oxford University Press, 1967), p. 118.
70. *Ibid.*, p. 111.
71. *A Study of History*, X, 232. See also chapter 5 in *Acquaintances*.
72. *Ibid.*, I, 442.
73. *Civilization on Trial*, p. 221.
74. *Ibid.*, p. 190.
75. *Ibid.*
76. *Ibid.*, p. 191.
77. *A Study of History*, VI, 274, quoted in footnote.
78. *Ibid.*, XII, 133.
79. *Ibid.*, p. 51.

Chapter Two

1. Oswald Spengler, *The Decline of the West* (New York: Alfred A. Knopf, 1962), I, 104–7.
2. *Ibid.*, pp. 109–10.
3. *Ibid.*, p. 40.
4. *Ibid.*
5. *Ibid.*, II, 507.
6. *Ibid.*, p. 39.
7. *Ibid.*, pp. 166–67.
8. *A Study of History*, III, 222.
9. *Ibid.*, p. 382.
10. *Ibid.*, IV, 11.
11. *Ibid.*, pp. 11–12.
12. *Ibid.*, IX, 296–97.
13. E. H. Goddard and P. A. Gibbons, *Civilization or Civilizations* (New York: Boni and Liveright, 1926), p. 207.
14. F. C. S. Schiller, Introduction to *ibid.*, p. xiv.
15. *Ibid.*, p. xv.
16. Spengler, *op. cit.*, p. 267.
17. *Ibid.*, p. 368.
18. *Ibid.*, p. 327.
19. *A Study of History*, I, 1.
20. *Ibid.*, IX, 433–34.

21. Toynbee, *Change and Habit* (New York: Oxford University Press, 1966), p. 112.

22. *Ibid.*, p. 87.

23. *A Study of History*, III, 159.

24. *Ibid.*, p. 385.

25. *Ibid.*, IX, 757.

26. Robery Jay Lifton, *History and Human Survival* (New York: Random House, 1970), p. 314.

27. Toynbee, *Civilization on Trial* and *The World and the West*, p. 235.

28. *Ibid.*, p. 236.

29. *Ibid.*, p. 271.

30. *Ibid.*, p. 257.

31. *Ibid.*, p. 266.

32. *Ibid.*, p. 236.

33. Frantz Fanon, *The Wretched of the Earth* (New York: Grove Press, 1968), p. 35.

34. Sartre, Preface to *ibid.*, p. 17.

35. *A Study of History*, VIII, 574.

36. Fanon, *op. cit.*, p. 53.

37. *A Study of History*, VIII, 541.

38. *Ibid.*, p. 591.

39. Robert Jay Lifton, "Psychohistory," *Partisan Review*, no. I (1970), p. 27.

40. Jacques Ellul, *The Political Illusion* (New York: Alfred A. Knopf, 1967), p. 50.

41. Louis Kampf, *On Modernism* (Cambridge, Mass.: MIT Press, 1967), p. 325.

42. Leonard Woolf, *Downhill All the Way* (New York: Harcourt, Brace and World, 1967), p. 178.

43. *The Education of Henry Adams* (New York: The Modern Library, 1931), p. 501.

44. *A Study of History*, XII, 51–52.

45. *Ibid.*, p. 331.

46. *Ibid.*, p. 528.

47. *Civilization on Trial*, p. 228.

48. *A Study of History*, IX, 436.

49. *Civilization on Trial*, p. 32.

50. *A Study of History*, IX, 436.

51. Toynbee, *America and the World Revolution* (New York: Oxford University Press, 1962), p. 116.

52. *A Study of History*, IV, 108.

53. *Ibid.*, p. 122.

54. *Ibid.*, VI, 313.

55. *Ibid.*, IX, 436.

56. *Ibid.*, p. 465.
57. *Ibid.*, p. 644.
58. *Ibid.*, XII, 518.
59. Toynbee, *Cities on the Move* (New York: Oxford University Press, 1970), p. 247.
60. Adams, *op. cit.*, p. 498.
61. Toynbee, *America and the World Revolution*, p. 206.
62. *Ibid.*, pp. 116–17.
63. *Ibid.*, p. 103.
64. *Experiences*, pp. 261–62.
65. *Ibid.*, p. 231.
66. *Ibid.*, p. 233.
67. *Ibid.*, p. 236.
68. *Ibid.*, p. 237.
69. *Ibid.*, p. 263.
70. *Ibid.*, p. 238.
71. *Ibid.*, p. 264.
72. *America and the World Revolution*, p. 40.
73. *Ibid.*, p. 92.
74. *Ibid.*, p. 210.
75. *Ibid.*, p. 132.
76. *Ibid.*, p. 144.
77. *Playboy* Interview with Toynbee, April, 1967, p. 72.
78. *A Study of History*, XII, 525.
79. *Experiences*, p. 290.

The following comment by Toynbee is significant in light of what he has had to say in this chapter and also in light of what has happened in Washington since this comment appeared in June of 1973. The dateline is London, England.

The United States' business is also the world's business. This is one of the present facts of life, though it is a nuisance both for United States' citizens and for the 94 per cent of the planet's population who are aliens. . . . Therefore Watergate is the whole world's affair. The financial corruption that has been brought to light in connection with Watergate is sensational.

However, this is not the heart of Watergate. The legal and constitutional aspects are still more—far more—grave than the financial aspects. . . . For non-Americans, the strangest and most questionable feature of the Government of the United States is the President's political family. . . . It is notorious that the Vice President has little power, but the President, after his election, appoints a band of personal aides and advisers. These appointments are made by the President autocratically. The electorate has no say in this. Yet some of the President's personal minions have greater power *de facto* than any officer of the United States Government. . . . Down to the time of President Wilson and Colonel House, at least, the electorate elected Presidents, and the President chose advisers who, on the whole, deserved the confidence in their moral integrity that had been accorded them. . . .

America's political business seems now to have become "business" of the unacceptable kind. In all the so-called "developed" countries, and perhaps most of all in the United States, the standard of ethical conduct in "business" has sunk below the average standard in other kinds of social relations. The operators in the White House have recently included not only lawyers but men recruited from the "business" world, including men whose previous careers had been in advertising.

One cause of the decline of political morality in America is that this has now sunk to the lowest level of American "business" morality. Down to the level of business *(New York Times,* June 15, 1973, p. 35).

Chapter Three

1. "Toynbee Answers Ten Basic Questions," *New York Times Magazine,* February 20, 1956, p. 64.

2. *A Study of History,* IX, 563.

3. *Ibid.,* p. 596.

4. *Ibid.,* p. 597.

5. *Ibid.,* pp. 602–3.

6. Henri Bergson, *The Two Sources of Morality and Religion* (Garden City: Doubleday Anchor, 1954), p. 290.

7. *Ibid.,* p. 289.

8. Bertrand Russell, "A Life of Disagreement," *Atlantic Monthly,* August, 1952. pp. 53–54.

9. Lewis Mumford, *The Transformation of Man* (New York: Harpers, 1956), p. 209.

10. *A Study of History,* IV, 300.

11. *Ibid.,* p. 298.

12. *Ibid.,* p. 299.

13. *Ibid.,* IX, 252.

14. *Ibid.,* p. 257.

15. *Ibid.,* III, 167.

16. *Ibid.,* pp. 167–68.

17. *Ibid.,* IV, 462–63.

18. *Ibid.,* p. 500.

19. *Ibid.,* p. 503.

20. Mumford, *In the Name of Sanity* (New York: Harcourt, Brace, 1954), pp. 67–69.

21. *Ibid.,* p. 73.

22. Robert Jay Lifton, *Boundaries* (New York: Vintage Books, 1970), p. 73.

23. R. D. Laing, *The Politics of Experience* (New York: Ballantine Books, 1968), p. 58.

24. *Ibid.,* p. 120.

25. *A Study of History*, IV, 640.
26. *Ibid.*, pp. 641–42.
27. *Ibid.*, VII, 554.
28. *Ibid.*, VIII, 29.
29. *Ibid.*, IX, 408.
30. *Ibid.*, p. 409.
31. *Ibid.*, p. 521.
32. Toynbee, *Experiences*, p. 208.
33. *A Study of History*, IX, 523.
34. *Ibid.*, pp. 524–25.
35. *Ibid.*, p. 526.
36. *Civilization on Trial*, p. 127.
37. *A Study of History*, IX, 554–55.
38. *Ibid.*, p. 527.
39. Toynbee, "The Desert Hermits," *Horizon* 12, no. 2 (Spring, 1970), 27.

Chapter Four

1. *A Study of History*, VII, 420–22.
2. *Ibid.*, I, 41 n.
3. *Ibid.*, p. 56.
4. *Ibid.*, pp. 195–97.
5. *Ibid.*, V, 29.
6. *Ibid.*, III, 248.
7. *Ibid.*, p. 249.
8. Toynbee, "The Desert Hermits," p. 27.
9. *A Study of History*, V, 233.
10. *Ibid.*, p. 338.
11. *Ibid.*, III, 2–3.
12. *Ibid.*, p. 3.
13. *Ibid.*, p. 28.
14. *Ibid.*, pp. 87–88.
15. *Ibid.*, p. 93.
16. *Ibid.*, pp. 89–90.
17. *Ibid.*, IV, 7.
18. *Ibid.*, p. 127.
19. *Ibid.*, VII, 468.
20. *Ibid.*, p. 548.
21. Toynbee, "The Desert Hermits," p. 27.
22. Karl Mannheim, *Ideology and Utopia* (New York: Harcourt, Brace, 1936), pp. 10–11.
23. *Ibid.*, p. 118.
24. *Ibid.*, p. 159.

25. Mannheim, *Essays on the Sociology of Culture* (New York: Oxford University Press, 1956), pp. 117–18.

26. *Ibid.*

27. *A Study of History,* V, 153.

28. *Ibid.,* p. 154.

29. *Ibid.,* p. 155.

30. *Ibid.,* p. 158 n.

31. *Ibid.,* p. 159.

32. *Ibid.,* IX, 564–65.

33. Norman Mailer, *Of Fire on the Moon* (New York: Little, Brown, 1970), p. 129.

34. *A Study of History,* III, 204.

35. Paul Valery, *Reflections on the World Today* (New York: Pantheon, 1948), pp. 21–22.

36. Michael Harrington, *The Accidental Century* (New York: Macmillan, 1965), p. 124.

37. *A Study of History,* IX, 573.

38. *Ibid.,* p. 576.

39. *Ibid.,* p. 577.

40. *Ibid.,* IV, 193.

41. *Ibid.,* p. 198.

42. *Ibid.,* IX, 612–13.

43. *Ibid.,* pp. 756–57.

44. *Ibid.,* X, 126.

45. Toynbee, *Change and Habit,* p. 226.

46. *Ibid.*

47. Toynbee, "The Desert Hermits," p. 27.

48. Herbert Marcuse, *Eros and Civilization* (New York: Vintage Book, 1962,) p. vii.

49. Marcuse, *One-Dimensional Man* (Boston: Beacon Press, 1966), p. xv.

50. Harrington, *op. cit.,* p. 112.

51. Marcuse, *An Essay on Liberation* (Boston: Beacon Press, 1969), p. 60.

52. *A Study of History,* XII, 316.

53. Theodore Roszak, *The Making of a Counter Culture* (Garden City: Doubleday Anchor, 1969), p. 41.

54. *Ibid.,* p. 42.

55. Leonard Woolf, *Downhill All the Way,* p. 225.

Chapter Five

1. Edward Gibbon, *Autobiography* (London: J. M. Dent, Ltd., 1911), p. 1.

2. Adams, *The Education of Henry Adams,* p. 4.

3. Gibbon, *op. cit.*, p. 2.

4. Pieter Geyl, *Debates with Historians* (New York: Meridian Books, 1958), p. 181.

5. Martin Duberman, *The Uncompleted Past* (New York: Random House, 1969), p. 51.

6. A. J. P. Taylor, "Dr. Toynbee's Round Trip," *Manchester Guardian*, October 9, 1958, p. 10.

7. *Ibid.*

8. Marguerite Howe, "Two Prophets of the Absent God," *The Nation*, October 1, 1973, p. 315.

9. Raymond Aron, "Evidence and Inference in History," *Daedalus*, Fall, 1958, p. 32.

10. "Dr. Toynbee at 70," *Manchester Guardian*, April 16, 1959.

11. *A Study of History*, XII, 1.

12. *Ibid.*, p. 575.

13. *Ibid.*, p. 640.

14. *Ibid.*, p. 7.

15. *Ibid.*, p. 321.

16. *Ibid.*, p. 591 n.

17. *Ibid.*, p. 2.

18. I. N. Moody, "Toynbee and the Historians," *Commonweal*, June 23, 1961, p. 330.

19. *Ibid.*

20. William Dray, "Toynbee's Search for Historical Laws," *History and Theory* I, no. 1 (1960), 39.

21. Gerhard Masur, "The Intent of Toynbee's History," *The American Historical Review* 67, no. 1 (October, 1961), 79.

22. *A Study of History*, XII, 13–14.

23. Dray, *op. cit.*, p. 32.

24. *A Study of History*, XII, 243–44.

25. *Ibid.*, pp. 244–45.

26. *Ibid.*, p. 249.

27. Isaiah Berlin, "History and Theory: The Concept of Scientific History," *History and Theory* I, no. 1 (1960), 25.

28. *A Study of History*, XII, 129–30.

29. *Ibid.*, p. 130.

30. *Ibid.*, p. 248.

31. *Ibid.*, p. 633.

32. *Ibid.*, pp. 40–41.

33. AAAS Committee on the Scientific Promotion of Human Welfare, "Committee Report," *Science*, December 29, 1961, p. 2083.

34. *A Study of History*, XII, 249.

35. *Ibid.*, p. 575.

36. *Ibid.*, p. 577.

37. *Ibid.*, p. 578.

38. *Ibid.*, p. 143.

39. Frederick D. Wilhelmsen, "History, Toynbee, and the Modern Mind: Betrayal of the West," *Modern Age*, I (Summer, 1957), 33.

40. *A Study of History*, XII, 186.

41. *Ibid.*, p. 585.

42. *Ibid.*, pp. 587–90.

43. *Ibid.*, p. 375.

44. *Ibid.*, p. 392.

45. *Ibid.*, p. 376.

46. Berlin, *op. cit.*, p. 30.

47. Kenneth Keniston, "Social Change and Youth in America," *Daedalus*, Winter, 1962, p. 170.

48. *A Study of History*, XII, 591.

49. *Ibid.*, pp. 629–30 n.

50. *Ibid.*, pp. 51–52.

51. *Ibid.*, p. 527.

52. *Ibid.*, p. 531.

53. *Ibid.*, p. 532.

54. Toynbee, *Civilization on Trial* and *The World and the West*, p. 243.

55. *A Study of History*, XII, 536.

56. *Ibid.*, p. 537.

57. *Ibid.*, p. 542.

58. C. P. Snow, *The Two Cultures and the Scientific Revolution* (New York: Cambridge University Press, 1959); Robert L. Heilbroner, *The Future as History* (New York: Harpers, 1960).

59. *A Study of History*, XII, 546.

60. *Ibid.*, p. 535.

61. Clark Kerr, *et al.*, *Industrialism and Industrial Man* (Cambridge: Harvard University Press, 1960), p. 28.

62. *Ibid.*, p. 282.

63. Erich Fromm, *May Man Prevail?* (Garden City: Anchor Books, 1961), p. 215.

64. *A Study of History*, XII, 477.

65. Masur, *op. cit.*, p. 80.

66. *A Study of History*, XII, 59.

67. *Ibid.*, p. 623.

68. *Ibid.*, p. 627.

69. *Ibid.*, p. 211.

70. *Ibid.*, p. 295.

71. *Ibid.*, p. 296.

72. *Ibid.*, p. 300.

73. *Ibid.*, p. 490.

74. *Ibid.*, p. 512.

75. *Ibid.*, pp. 595–98.

76. "Rabbis Rebuke Toynbee," Editorial, *Christian Century*, June 14, 1961, p. 733.

77. Jacob B. Agus, "Toynbee's Epistle to the Jews," *Commentary*, 32, no. 3 (September, 1961), 239.

78. *Ibid.*, p. 242.

79. *Ibid.*, p. 241.

80. *Ibid.*, p. 242.

81. Moody, *op. cit.*, p. 332.

82. *A Study of History*, XII, 407.

83. *Ibid.*, p. 461.

84. *Ibid.*, p. 616.

85. *Ibid.*, p. 264.

86. *Ibid.*, p. 306.

87. *Ibid.*, p. 343.

88. "Toynbee Revisited," *Time*, May 12, 1961, p. 89.

89. Geoffrey Bruun, "Challenge and Response," *Saturday Review*, May 27, 1961n p. 17.

90. Moody, *op. cit.*, p. 332.

Chapter Six

1. Gibbon, *Atuobiography*, pp. 150–51.

2. Toynbee, *Experiences*, p. 368.

3. Toynbee, *Civilization on Trial*, pp. 202–3.

4. Herbert J. Muller, "The Pride and Prejudice of Toynbee," *The New Republic*, September 10, 1956, p. 17.

5. Walter Kaufmann, "Toynbee's Study of History," *Partisan Review*, Fall, 1955, p. 541.

6. Christopher Dawson, "Toynbee's Study of History," *International Affairs* 31 (April, 1955), 158.

7. *A Study of History*, X, 5.

8. *Civilization on Trial*, p. 146.

9. *A Study of History*, X, 307.

10. Toynbee, *Change and Habit*, p. 26.

11. *Ibid.*, p. 73.

12. *A Study of History*, X, 3.

13. *Ibid.*, IX, 347.

14. *Ibid.*, VII, 444.

15. *Ibid.*, p. 419.

16. *Ibid.*, pp. 420–22.

17. *Ibid.*, p. 526.

18. C. G. Jung, *Psychological Types* (London: Kegan Paul, Trench Trubner, Ltd., 1946), p. 556.

19. *A Study of History*, IX, 327–28.

20. *Ibid.*, VII, 500–1.

21. *Acquaintances,* p. 179.

22. Toynbee's essay "The Genesis of Pollution," *New York Times,* September 16, 1973, does not seem designed to win him many friends on the religious side. Toynbee traces our overconsumption, our pollution, back to Genesis when God advised men to have dominion over the earth and to multiply.

23. *A Study of History,* XII, 71.

24. *Change and Habit,* p. 110.

25. *Experiences,* p. 128.

26. "Playboy Interview: Arnold Toynbee," *Playboy,* April, 1967, p. 74.

27. *Experiences,* pp. 134–143.

28. *Ibid.,* p. 127.

29. *Ibid.,* p. 143.

30. *Ibid.,* pp. 146–49.

31. *Ibid.,* p. 369.

32. Toynbee, *An Historian's Approach to Religion* (New York; Oxford University Press, 1967), p. 253.

33. *Ibid.,* pp. 298–99.

Selected Bibliography

The works of Toynbee may be grouped in several ways: the following would seem to be the simplest way to categorize his writings:
1. Reports dealing with his wartime work with British intelligence
2. A *Study of History*
3. Studies relating to the Graeco-Roman world
4. Books with a religious dimension
5. His work at Chatham House
6. Travel books
7. Autobiography
8. General works in which the concern is primarily with the contemporary.

By whatever standards or tastes one may wish to evaluate these writings, one can—granting the limitations, the errors, the prejudices—only conclude that we have in Arnold Toynbee a magnitude, a cosmic quality, and an expertise that staggers the imagination and challenges the endurance of the reader. The total effect is that of a twentieth-century intellectual monument.

1. Books by Arnold Toynbee

Nationality and the War. London: J. M. Dent, 1915.
The Treatment of Armenians in the Ottoman Empire 1915–16. London: Sir Joseph Caustion and Sons, 1916.
Belgian Deportations. London: T. F. Unwin, 1917.
The German Terror in Belgium. New York: George H. Doran, 1917.
The German Terror in France. New York: Hodder and Stoughton, 1917.
The Western Question in Greece and Turkey. New York: H. Fertig, 1923.
The World After the Peace Conference, New York: Oxford University Press, 1925.
A Study of History. Vol. I, Introduction, The Geneses of Civilizations. New York: Oxford University Press, 1934.
    Vol. II, *The Geneses of Civilizations*, 1934.
    Vol. III, *The Growths of Civilizations*, 1934.
    Vol. IV, *The Breakdowns of Civilizations*, 1939.
    Vol. V, *The Disintegrations of Civilizations*, 1939.

Vol. VI, *The Disintegrations of Civilizations,* 1939.

Civilization on Trial. New York: Oxford University Press, 1948.

The World and the West, New York: Oxford University Press, 1953.

A Study of History. Vol. VII, *Universal States and Universal Churches.* New York; Oxford University Press, 1954.

   Vol. VIII, *Heroic Ages: Contacts between Civilizations in Space,* 1954.

   Vol. IX, *Contacts between Civilizations in Time, Law and Freedom in History, and The Prospects of Western Civilization,* 1954.

   Vol. X, *The Inspirations of Historian: A Note on Chronology,* 1954.

An Historian's Approach to Religion. New York: Oxford University Press, 1956.

Christianity Among the Religions of the World. New York: Scribner, 1957.

East to West: A Journey Round the World. New York: Oxford University Press, 1958.

Hellenism: The History of a Civilization. New York: Oxford University Press, 1959.

A Study of History. Vol. XI, *Historical Atlas and Gazetteer,* with Edward D. Myers, New York: Oxford University Press, 1959.

A Study in History. Vol. XII, *Reconsiderations,* New York: Oxford University Press, 1961.

Between Oxus and Jumna. New York: Oxford University Press, 1961.

America and the World Revolution. New York: Oxford University Press, 1962.

Between Niger and Nile. New York: Oxford University Press, 1965.

Hannibal's Legacy: The Hannibalic War's Effect on Roman Life. Two Volumes. New York: Oxford University Press, 1965.

Change and Habit: The Challenge of Our Time. New York: Oxford University Press, 1966.

Acquaintances. New York: Oxford University Press, 1967.

Between Maule and Amazon. New York: Oxford University Press, 1967.

Experiences. New York: Oxford University Press, 1969.

Some Problems of Greek History. New York: Oxford University Press, 1969.

Cities on the Move. New York: Oxford University Press, 1970.

Surviving the Future. New York: Oxford University Press, 1971.

Constantine Porphyrogenitus and His World. New York: Oxford University Press, 1973.

2. Books edited by Arnold Toynbee

Twelve Men of Action in Graeco-Roman History. Boston: Beacon Press, 1952.

Cities of Destiny. New York: McGraw-Hill, 1967.

The Crucible of Christianity. Cleveland: World, 1969.

3. Books coauthored by Arnold Toynbee

Forbes, Nevill; Toynbee, Arnold J.; Mitrany, D.; and Hogarth, D. G. *The Balkans.* London: Oxford University Press, 1915.
Toynbee, Arnold J.; and Boultner, V. M. *Abyssinia and Italy.* New York: Johnson Reprint, 1936.
Toynbee, Arnold, and Toynbee, Veronica. *Survey of International Affairs.* New York: Oxford University Press, 1967.
Toynbee, Arnold J.; and Urban, G. R. *Toynbee on Toynbee.* New York: Oxford University Press, 1974.

4. Abridgments or Selections from Toynbee

D. C. Somervell. *A Study of History.* Abridgment of volumes I to VI. New York: Oxford University Press, 1946.
D. C. Somervell. *A Study of History.* Abridgment of volumes VII to X. New York: Oxford University Press, 1957.
Fowler, Albert V., ed. *War and Civilization.* New York: Oxford University Press, 1950.

5. Critiques of Toynbee

DAWSON, CHRISTOPHER. *Dynamics of World History.* Edited by John J. Mulloy. New York: Sheed and Ward, 1956.
Christopher Dawson writes history in the grand manner. He comes to history from the religious position of Roman Catholicism. One chapter in this book carries the title "The Problem of Metahistory." According to Dawson, "Metahistory is concerned with the nature of history, the meaning of history and the cause and significance of historical change" (p. 287). One would expect Toynbee's name to surface in a chapter on metahistory, and it does. To Dawson, Spengler and Toynbee are the modern representatives of metahistory: "They are the bugbears of the academic historians" (p. 290). Dawson accepts Toynbee's definition of a civilization as an intelligible field for historical study. (Later Toynbee denied this himself.)

If historians are to object to Toynbee as a metahistorian, then, Dawson says, they must not do so on the grounds of Toynbee's system, but "because he has attempted too much with insufficient material" (p. 291). Dawson finds Toynbee indifferent to a comparative study of culture. There is this possible objection: it may be that Toynbee is writing sociology and not history (p. 291). It would be my guess that sociologists would be even more quick to reject Toynbee as a sociologist than historians have been to dismiss him as an historian.

One chapter was written right after the tenth volume of *A Study* came off the presses: "One cannot lightly pass judgment on a work of 6,000 pages which has been written with so much erudition and conviction. Nor can one get much help from the judgment of others working in the same field, for they hardly exist, at least in England" (p. 390). Dawson points out that the book has not been well received because it deals with civilizations and this is not the proper unit for historical study. Dawson confesses that the early volumes left him perplexed: Toynbee was a moral absolutist in his judgments, and as theorist he was a cultural relativist. That big switch in volume VII was a bit too much for Dawson to swallow. Toynbee went from a "relativist phenomenology of equivalent cultures" to a "unitary philosophy of history" comparable to the idealist philosophers of the nineteenth century (pp. 392–93).

Dawson is sympathetic to Toynbee's view that civilizations exist to serve religion and "not religion to serve civilization." However, writes Dawson, "Dr. Toynbee's reduction of history to theology" will not make him any more popular with theologians than it has with historians. Dawson's position is that "religions must be studied theologically" (p. 398).

Christopher Dawson concludes his essay on Toynbee in a kind manner. The telescopic survey of history has its value, "especially when it is carried out by a scholar of immense learning and universal cultural interest like Dr. Toynbee." The historian and the social anthropologist cannot read *A Study* "without gaining new insights" into the relations between civilizations.

FRANKEL, CHARLES. *The Case for Modern Man.* Boston: Beacon Press, 1959.

Frankel's purpose in writing this book is to show how certain thinkers are belittling man's reason; thinkers who are working against our liberal traditions, who are doom-oriented in regard to the contemporary West. Four men are singled out as enemies of liberalism and science: Jacques Maritain, who condemns the liberal for his espousal of experimentation in morals; Reinhold Niebuhr, who rejects human perfectibility; Karl Mannhein, who denies belief in objectivity; and Arnold Toynbee, who denies man the right to build his civilization on secular humanistic foundations (p. 5). These four men suggest that we are at the end of the liberal era; they reject the liberal vision of human history.

Frankel's chapter on Toynbee begins, as so many comments on Toynbee do, with respectful remarks about his erudition. Toynbee is a man "who has surveyed the course of every human civilization on record." No other history rests on "so much erudition." *A Study* is a "singular achievement on the present intellectual landscape" (pp. 164–65). But again as often, one pays his respects and then promptly tears into the erudite Dr. Toynbee. (1) To Frankel, Toynbee's history with its pre-determined sequence turns history into astrology. There are too many contingencies for the Toynbee system. Reality is more plural than Toynbee would lead us to believe. (2) Each civilization is compressed into the same shape. Frankel cannot accept this. (3) Once more we find Toynbee's religious bias at the center of intellectual differences. *A Study* makes quick play of Gibbon and Voltaire and what they represent in the West and asks us to return to St. Augustine. Frankel cannot stomach Toynbee's notion that a liberal society cannot be secure and progressive so long as it operates on secular moral postulates and that must somehow have a higher religion as a stabilizing force (p. 193). (4) *A Study* is the work of a Victorian who is hostile to our technology (p. 192). (5) Toynbee's book never offers a social policy; rather what we get is "a flight from social policy." Instead of controlling our destiny by reason and science and social policy, we are asked to place our trust in "the coming of a new breed of men who will bring a miraculous vision with them." Toynbee's work is an "instrument for denigrating social analysis" (p. 194).

In short, Charles Frankel sees Toynbee as opposed to modern man and to the democratic liberalism some men have come to cherish. Astrology and saints are not exactly assurances of salvation—or even of continued existence.

GARGAN, EDWARD T., ed. *The Intent of Toynbee's History.* Chicago: Loyola University Press, 1961.

This book, along with the one edited by Ashley Montagu, gives us much of the material Toynbee refers to in *Reconsiderations.* In a sense, the Montagu book affords the reader a series of general critiques of Toynbee, whereas in the Gargan book one gets critiques written by specialists. That is to say, in Montagu the critics whatever may be their own expertise adopt a general view, and in the Gargan book the experts criticize Toynbee from the position of their own specialty.

The Intent of Toynbee's History is the result of a symposium held at Loyola University in November, 1955. Toynbee wrote the preface to the book, and, as always, he is generous. The author and his critics share a common purpose: to make a tiny contribution to "mankind's common-stock of knowledge and understanding." The encounter between the author and the critic is the equivalent of the medieval disputation. The critic does what a traffic policeman does for traffic: he helps to keep it moving. In the preface, Toynbee wrote: "The nine appraisals in the present book are some of the most valuable and constructive of all the critiques that I have received; and it would have been a great loss for me if I had had to go to press without being able to take full account of these" (p. iv).

The nine essays are:

William H. McNeill, "Some Basic Assumptions of Toynbee's *A Study of History*."

Friedrich Engel-Janosi, "Toynbee and the Tradition of Universal History."

David M. Robinson, "The Historical Validity of Toynbee's Approach to the Greco-Roman World."

G. E. von Grunebaum. "Toynbee's Concept of Islamic Civilization."

Hans Kohn, "Toynbee and Russia."

Matthew A. Fitzsimons, "Toynbee's Approach to the History and Character of the United States."

Edward Rochie Hardy, "The Historical Validity of Toynbee's Approach to Universal Churches."

Eric Voegelin, "Toynbee's History as a Search for Truth."

Oscar Halecki, "The Validity of Toynbee's Conception of the Prospects of Western Civilization."

Rather than making anything like an itemized list of criticisms from the Gargan book, I should like to single out a few somewhat random comments. McNeill, as with so many others, finds Toynbee's professed empiricism "largely a pose": "The heart of Toynbee's intellectual procedure has always been the sudden flash of insight" (p. 40). His procedure is insight and imagination rather than "arguments and induction." And one will discover that at critical points Toynbee will resort to myths and metaphors (p. 42). McNeill writes: "I find much scintillating suggestion and stimulation in Toynbee's pages; he has opened vistas of history and put questions before me as no other single author has done. For this I am grateful, and insofar as he does the like for others of the historical profession, we should all be grateful" (p. 45).

The essay by Engel-Janosi is helpful in that he gives us the names of others who have worked in the tradition of universal history. Among them are Thucydides, Polybius, Bishop of Hippo, Anselm, Otto of Freysing, Vico, Gibbon, Comte, Ranke, and Hegel.

Toynbee, the generalist, is inclined to overlook the specific. Robinson holds that he neglects the "specialized disciplines necessary to the historian of broad view" (p. 84). Fitzsimons says Toynbee neglects politics and the short-range decisions statesmen have to make (pp. 139–41). Over and over Toynbee is so busy with his grand parallels and historical similarities that "he is almost unable to see an event in itself" (p. 147). One seems to get an aura of erudition but nothing very concrete.

There is so much religion in *A Study* that Hardy's remarks are especially timely. Hardy finds three levels of knowledge about religion: (1) that of the practicing believer; (2) that of the student of original sources; and (3) that of the cursory reader (p. 162). A man can know only one religion "from the inside," and this condition tends to lead to distortions in what Toynbee has to say about religion. Judaism again becomes a thorn. "Toynbee seems to be more annoyed than anything else with

Jewish history." It is "Judaism's concreteness and recalcitrance to classification that gets in his way" (p. 169).

Voegelin accuses Toynbee of a "dilettantism with regard to questions of reason and revelation, philosophy and revelation, metaphysics and theology, intuition and science, as well as communication, that could be easily overcome by anybody who wanted to overcome it" (p. 197).

This book carries harsh and penetrating comments about Toynbee; but as usual we find tempering admiration for his scholarship, for his immense effort—and each writer seems in one way or another to recognize Toynbee as an engaging personality.

GEYL, PIETER. *Debates with Historians.* New York: Meridian Books, 1958.

While many of the world's famous scholars have written about Arnold Toynbee in one fashion or another, the most important commentary on Toynbee has probably come from Pieter Geyl, longtime professor of modern history at the University of Utrecht. This volume "debates" with such historians as Isaiah Berlin, Carlyle, Macauley, Michelet, Ranke, and Sorokin. It is a book of twelve chapters and four of them deal with Toynbee: 5, "Toynbee's System of Civilization" (also in Montagu's book); 6, "Prophets of Doom: Sorokin and Toynbee"; 7, "Toynbee Once More: Empiricism or Apriorism"; and 8, "Toynbee the Prophet: The Last Four Volumes."

Geyl begins chapter 5 on a generous and complimentary note. Toynbee, he says, belongs to a noble group who have tried to "survey history as a whole," and he is not the least among them. Toynbee's reading and learning are "almost without precedent." He moves at ease through ancient and modern civilizations, he is profoundly familiar with classical literature, and he knows the Bible as few historians have. He writes in a "splendid, full, and supple style." *A Study* is a "majestic vision." His is a "remarkable mind, unusual in our everyday world of historians" (pp. 109–10).

However, for all these words of sincere praise, Geyl is no admirer of Toynbee *in toto*. Among his criticisms are these. (1) Toynbee's system in the end, grand as it is, "seems to me useless." (2) The major criticism that encompasses all the others has to do with Toynbee's professed empirical method. Toynbee is deceiving himself, for "he selects the instances which will support his theses, or he presents them in a way that suits him" (p. 116). (3) Toynbee's erudition is protective. He deals with historical places and periods where it is "difficult to check him." (4) One of Toynbee's pet peeves is nationalism, and this posture on his part is one of the favorite areas from which to launch criticisms against him. Geyl holds that Toynbee lacks an understanding of the national state and that his inability to appreciate national states leads to historical error. This animosity to nationalism "constitutes one of the serious shortcomings" of *A Study* (p. 147). (5) Toynbee's thesis that the West is in trouble is something which does not set too well with Geyl: The West need not be "frightened by his darkness." We need not accept the "downward course" Toynbee has assigned us Westerners. We can have confidence that "the future lies open before us" (p. 149). (6) Geyl holds that Toynbee is confining our prospects excessively when our salvation can only be bought by "a return to the Christian religion." If this were indeed the case, then Toynbee has given us "a sentence of death" (p. 159). (7) Geyl doesn't like Toynbee's attitude toward other historians: "He is inclined to deal somewhat contemptuously with them" (p. 161). (8) To the Dutch historian, the English historian simply failed to consider "the infinite complexity" which is the stuff of history, Toynbee's system is forever getting in the way, and that system is an irrational one. (9) Especially annoying to Geyl is Toynbee's indifference to the West. "Western civilization means nothing to him" (p. 185). As a consequence he is unmindful of the contributions of science. (10) Toynbee indulges in excessive simplicity. In despair, Geyl asks, "Is it possible more recklessly to simplify?" (p. 175).

Finally, Geyl's conclusion is direct: Toynbee is not an historian; rather he is a prophet. The final line of Toynbee in *Debates with Historians* is the following: "I regard his prophecy as a blasphemy against Western civilization" (p 202). Again, then, Toynbee has drawn onto himself the harsh words of a distinguished historian.

MONTAGU, M. F. ASHLEY, ed. *Toynbee and History.* Boston: Porter Sargent, 1956.

If a reader had to choose one book of commentary on Arnold Toynbee, then this book would probably be the best choice. The list of contributors is impressive: the opinions are varied, with the unfavorable ones quite definitely enjoying a numerical advantage. Three of the essays are by Toynbee himself.

Montagu's foreword is given to superlatives. For example, he writes that *A Study* "is undoubtedly the most widely known work of contemporary historical scholarship." "Without exaggeration," this book is one of "the most famous and most widely discussed books of its time." Toynbee is "a power in the world to reckon with," an achievement of "staggering proportions" (p. vii). The ten volumes add up to 6,290 pages, 3,150,000 words, 332 pages of index with 19,000 entries (p viii).

I would echo Montagu's thought: "It is scarcely possible that there is anyone living who, from the matrix of his own knowledge, could deliver an authoritative verdict on the work as a whole—such polymaths are no longer among us" (p. viii). But if no one person can render this verdict, the contributors to this volume render quite specific verdicts on sectors of the whole; and a reader will encounter substantial summaries of major theses from Toynbee.

Toynbee has the final word in this book: "I do not mind being called a minor historian, so long as it is not understood that I am not renouncing the right to study history and to write some, too, when I choose. I have this right, like anyone else. It is one of our freedoms" (p. 385).

The contributors to *Toynbee and History* are of such prominence that one can do them justice only by listing each and the title of his essay.

1. Arnold Toynbee, "A *Study of History:* What I am Trying to Do"
2. Arnold Toynbee, "A *Study of History:* What the Book Is For, How the Book Took Shape"
3. Tangye Lean, "A Study of Toynbee"
4. Pieter Geyl, "Toynbee's System of Civilizations"
5. G. J. Renier, "Toynbee's *Study of History*"
6. H. Mitchell, "Herr Spengler and Mr. Toynbee"
7. Sir Ernest Barker, "Dr. Toynbee's *Study of History*, A Review"
8. *Times Literary Supplement,* "Study of Toynbee: A Personal View of History"
9. Lawrence Stone, "Historical Consequences and Happy Families"
10. A. J. P. Taylor, "Much Learning"
11. Geoffrey Barraclough, "The Prospects of the Western World"
12. Hugh Trevor-Roper, "Testing the Toynbee System"
13. W. H. Walsh, "The End of a Great Work"
14. Christopher Dawson, "The Place of Civilization in History"
15. Lewis Mumford, "The Napoleon of Notting Hill"
16. Rushton Coulborn, "Fact and Fiction in Toynbee's *Study of History*"
17. George Catlin, "Toynbee's *Study of History*"
18. Pitirim A. Sorokin, "Toynbee's Philosophy of History"
19. Hans Morgenthau, "Toynbee and the Historical Imagination"
20. Kenneth W. Thompson, "Toynbee's Approach to History"
21. W. den Boer, "Toynbee and Classical History: Historiography and Myth"
22. Wayne Altree, "Toynbee's Treatment of Chinese History"
23. Gotthold Weil, "Arnold Toynbee's Conception of the Future of Islam"
24. O. H. K. Spate, "Reflections on Toynbee's *A Study of History:* A Geographer's View"
25. Walter Kaufmann, "Toynbee and Super-History"
26. Frederick E. Robin, "The Professor and the Fossil"
27. Abba Eban, "the Toynbee Heresy"
28. Linus Walker, "Toynbee and Religion: A Catholic View"
29. Jan Romein, "Reason or Religion: An Old Dispute Renewed"
30. Hans Kohn, "Faith and a Vision of a Universal History"

MULLER, HERBERT J. *The Uses of the Past.* New York: New American
Library, 1954.

One will find numerous references to Toynbee in Muller's *The Loom
of History* (1958), and in *Freedom in the Ancient World* (1961); but it is
in *The Uses of the Past* that Muller most generously discusses Toynbee.
We find our first and a key difference with Toynbee before we get
beyond the short preface. Muller finds *A Study* "a remarkable bold, rich,
stimulating work . . . the most impressive historical work of our time."
Muller explains its popularity on the basis of our desire to find salvation;
and salvation is what Toynbee has to offer. He seems to be saying over
and over: a miracle will save us. Muller grants that Toynbee may be
right, but we "had better not live on this assumption." There is no firm
evidence in *A Study* that prayer will save us, and Muller's counsel is
that, if we want to save our world, we had better use our heads.

There are futher points where Muller parts company with Toynbee. (1)
Byzantium: "it does not fit into the neat cyclical patterns of Spengler,
Toynbee or Sorokin" (p. 27). (2) Rome: Muller pointedly rejects
Toynbee's position that Rome is "merely a phase of Hellenic society."
Rome has a place in history which is peculiarly its own (p. 203). (3) Concept of empire: Toynbee's thesis that empire status is a sign of decadence
is too simplistic and historically inaccurate. An empire may be a sign of
genuine accomplishment and growth (p. 221). (4) Humanism: Muller
cannot accept Toynbee's dismissal of humanism. One gathers that Muller
never quite forgives Toynbee for thinking that if the West should be
blown skyhigh with the bomb, then we might see some Negrito Pygmies
start us on the road again because they were God-believing folk.

Muller observes that "the great historians, from Herodotus to Toynbee, have generally been distinguished for their imaginative reach and
grasp, not necessarily the soundess of their conclusions" (pp. 36–37).
Surely, Toynbee's "imaginative reach and grasp" compare favorably with
those of any historian, ancient or modern.

ORTEGA Y GASSET, JOSE. *An Interpretation of Universal History.* Trans-
lated by Mildred Adams. New York: W. W. Norton, 1973.

This volume is an uneven and uncertain effort compiled from a lecture
course on Toynbee given in 1948–49. It lacks the coherence and fine
style we find in other books by Ortega y Gasset. Furthermore, the contents deal much more with the ideas of the lecturer than with the ideas
of Arnold Toynbee. Yet it is significant that a man of world prominence
should give a course on Toynbee—even if largely to refute Toynbee. Or-

tega y Gasset tags Toynbee as belonging to "the new profession of inter-
nationalist." Indeed, Toynbee is the "most eminent representative" of
this profession. Ortega also charges Toynbee with the following faults.
(1) *A Study of History* is a misnomer. It is not a study of history but a
philosophy of history (p. 26). But Toynbee is no philosopher. "He does
not launch himself on the high sea of ultimate principles; his navigation
is purely that of the pilot boat, and this is bad" (pp. 250–51). He is in
philosophical matters "a man of enchanting and paradisiacal innocence"
(p. 279). (2) Toynbee is engaging in hypothesis, not empirical method
(p. 240). He is accused of "the childishness of his resistance to fact" (p. 251).
Toynbee is one "who never yields to facts" (p. 245). He is not "a man of
reason, of science, of theory." He is a man who believes in "a strange
mysticism about history." (3) Toynbee's classical bias is excessive: "he
drains each people of its own peculiar history and fills the hole with the
unique Greco-Roman history which he finds repeated in all the rest"
(p. 127). (4) One might get the impression that Toynbee is so English that
he thinks the English "were chosen by God to invent everything." Yet in
all of Toynbee, "there is not a single word that praises the English"
(p. 231). (5) Toynbee suffers a "misplaced preacher's passion" which, Ortega
says, leads to results that are "ridiculous," "insolent," and "calamitous"
(p. 253). His talent is not that of science, "but of belief, of closed faith"
(p. 252).

In Ortega, Toynbee comes out as an acrobat at twisting facts, a man
given to intellectual tricks, whose primary theory is a "mixture of geography and phantasmagoria." Toynbee is trying "to light a small candle on
our obscure destinies" (p 252). *A Study of History* is a magnificent failure, if we may believe Ortega y Gasset. There are major historical errors, philosophical superficiality, and some Spanish words that Toynbee
just does not understand. It is "an ocean of typography through which
navigation is long and painful" (p. 37).

One can only wonder: had Ortega y Gasset been around to read the
full *A Study*, would he have written such a petulant book?

POPPER, KARL R. *The Open Society and Its Enemies*. Princeton, N.J.:
    Princeton University Press, 1950.
Karl Popper has an immense respect for Toynbee. He admires his
ideas; and he feels Toynbee is so superior to Spengler that he is reluctant to mention the two of them in the same context. Yet for all this respect, he refers to Alfred North Whitehead and Toynbee as the two
foremost irrationalist authorities of our century. Popper is rather specific
in some of his differences with Toynbee.
(1)He finds him much too indifferent to science and scientists. Only
Einstein gets mentioned in the first six volumes of *A Study*. (2) He cannot accept Toynbee's notion that civilizations are "born, grow, break

down, and die" (p. 505). (3) There is a mysticism which annoys Popper. ". . .mysticism attempts to rationalize the irrational, and at the same time it seeks the mystery in the wrong place" (p. 431). (4) He is irritated by what he calls Toynbee's reluctance to take "arguments seriously." This leads to an intellectualism "which expresses its disillusionment . . . of a rational solution of our social problems, by an escape into a religious mysticism" (p. 436). (5) Toynbee is too religious, too much in search of the transcendent. Toynbee "claims that only allegiance to a superhuman whole can save us" (p. 442). To Popper, the idea that God reveals Himself in history is nothing less than "blasphemy" (p. 455). (6) The author of *A Study* is too prone to the universal. "There is no history of mankind, there is only an indefinite number of histories of all kinds of aspects of human life" (p. 453). (7) Historicism, in whatever guise, is an enemy of the open society. Historicism, in brief, is the idea that men are caught up in some historical sweep—a movement transcending the lives of individual men. In the Popper context, Toynbee is the consummate historicist. "For to progress is to move towards some kind of end, towards an end which exists for us a human beings. 'History' cannot do that; only we, the human individuals, can do it" (p. 463).

Finally, Popper views *A Study* as Toynbee's *tour de force* to escape via a time machine into the past. A general criticism of Toynbee runs through many of the pages of *The Open Society and Its Enemies:* Toynbee is taken to task for failing to offer solutions to real practical problems in the real world. In Popper, Toynbee joins a distinguished group of enemies of the open society: Plato, Aristotle, Hegel, Marx, and Whitehead.

SAMUEL, MAURICE *The Professor and the Fossil*. New York: Knopf, 1956.

BERKOWITZ, E. *Judaism: Fossil or Ferment*. New York: Philosophical Library, 1956.

Toynbee refers to the Judaic faith as a fossil—and this has led to these two books plus many articles. Abba Eban holds that Toynbee never tells us what he means by "fossil." "The concept is never defined. It is indeed a basic weakness of his work that it evades the definitions of its fundamental terms" ("The Toynbee Heresy," in Montagu, *Toynbee and History*, p. 324). Eban goes on to say that Toynbee presents Jewish history as "a grotesque psychic aberration." Toynbee portrays the State of Israel as "a squalid little Ghetto without grace or meaning." The persecution of Jews in Nazi Germany becomes less tragic than the plight of 750,000 homeless but alive Arabs (p. 326).

When we turn to Samuel's book we find three kinds of criticism leveled at *A Study:* (1) Samuel feels it lacks intelligibility. He finds what he calls "the Blurring Effect" which leaves the reader under the impression "that a point has been made when it has actually been avoided in a welter of words." (2) His second contention with Toynbee is the historian's carelessness with historical facts. (3) Finally, he criticizes the way Toynbee treats some contemporary happenings in Jewish life (p. 17). When Toynbee is in error, he does not make a retraction, a modification, or a confession of error (p. 101). Samuel says he does not expect the historian "to know the truth; I only want him to be truthful" (p. 267).

Samuel does not take kindly to the religious posturings of the author of *A Study*, who is a fundamentalist Christian when it squares with his thesis or theses, but who is mostly commonly a "religious relativist." Also he finds a struggle going on in Toynbee between his Christian pacifism and his admiration for the Pagan warrior of ancient Greece (p. 138).

Berkowitz, Eban, and Samuel all go to great lengths to refute Toynbee's categorizing the Judaic faith as a fossil religion. Toynbee's laborious efforts to look at these challenges is found in *Recollections* (pp. 477–517). He does agonize, but I fear he scarcely satisfies many of his Jewish critics.

"The Contribution of Arnold Toynbee." *Diogenes.* Number 13, Spring, 1956.

The whole issue is devoted to Toynbee. In the foreword by Roger Caillois one may read comments such as these: "With Toynbee, history definitely ceases to be local or national" (p 4) and "The greatness of Toynbee is to have understood and to have made others understand that the era of one's own hearth is over" (p. 5).

The contents include:

Arnold J. Toynbee, "*A Study of History:* What I Am Trying To Do"
Lewis Mumford, "*A Study of History*"
Jacques Madaule, "A Biological and Mystical Interpretation of History: Arnold J. Toynbee"
Kenneth W. Thompson, "Toynbee and World Politics"
Lewis Renou, "The Civilization of India According to Arnold Toynbee"
Robert Heine-Geldern, "The Origin of Ancient Civilizations and Toynbee's Theories"

6. Bibliography of Criticisms in *Reconsiderations*

The reader who wants an exhaustive listing of critiques of Toynbee's books can turn to the Bibliography at the end of *Reconsiderations*, XII, 680–90. This list contains over 200 references; and while it is limited to articles and books cited in vol. XII, it is a fairly adequate accounting of the criticism which has been directed at *A Study of History*. Many of the references are to the volumes edited by Ashley Montagu and Edward Gargan. To duplicate this extensive bibliography seems beyond the needs of this present work. There is considerable advantage if one has a concern for these various criticisms in turning to *Reconsiderations,* for there one can easily find how Toynbee responds to virtually each one of these commentaries. One thing should be noted: Toynbee frequently uses footnotes for his most significant responses.

7. Note on Indexes

Indexing is serious business with Toynbee and in recent years he has entrusted this assignment to Mrs. Toynbee. The length of the various indexes is commensurate with the voluminousness of Toynbee's writings. Volume III caries the index for the first three volumes of *A Study;* volume VI for the next three volumes; volume X for VII–X. Volume XI is an atlas and gazetteer for all ten volumes of *A Study.* The index in volume X runs to 179 pages. The atlas and gazetteer is a volume of 257 pages, larger in format than the other volumes. There is also a consolidated index for the *Survey of International Affairs.*

Index